Go @#$% Yourself!

An Ungentlemanly Disagreement

between the author

FILIPPO ARGENTI

and the modern day nanny state

Foreword by Corso Donati, Esq.

Olympia Press

"Go @#$% Yourself!" - An Ungentlemanly Disagreement
OLYMPIA PRESS

Argenti, Filippo

ISBN: 978-1-60872-999-9
BOOK DESIGN BY Goodloe Byron
AN IMPRINT OF DISRUPTIVE PUBLISHING, INC.

17 DANTE 17

To my brother,

There is no way in hell I could have pulled this off without you.

also...

To Guido Cavalcanti,

Go fuck your stupid self.

Foreword

When I was first approached to review An Ungentlemanly Disagreement, I recognized its importance just as quickly as I recognized its author. Filippo "Silver" Argenti is a man whom I have known for many years: a prominent member to the prestigious Adimari family, a man of conviction--a 'convict' if you will--and a deeply devoted believer of things. He is a man who speaks his mind and minds what he speaks. He fights with his words and words are what he fights. He will grow into a force to be reckoned with if his opponents are not careful, which is why everyone on the planet should hearken Filippo Argenti.

Instead of Persia or Carthage, the great battlefields of our time are the streets that surround our own city halls. Too many nations have used these corridors to transform governments into fortresses: a grown-ups table that tells us to sit straight, to quietly chew our food, and ultimately to stay out of trouble [with them]. This doting governess which some call the "nanny state" has truly become a plague on both our houses, but I do not fear her and neither does Filippo Argenti. He understands that when a child grows up he obtains the power to discharge anyone in his service, especially tired, old nannies. He believes there is more to our lives than being told what to do, and more to adulthood than being treated like a child.

You, my Dear Reader, are not a child. We are all adults
here, and we all have the power to surrender this nanny.
What would that lead to? Who would be there to take care
of us?

I yield the floor and our future to Filippo Argenti.

—Corso Donati, Esq.

Book I: The Trivial
Grammar

I

"Knowledge is power."
– Old Timey saying

Could they be wrong about that?

One of the oldest stories in history is about a garden with a tree whose fruit ended up causing all that is wrong with the world. This tale tells in telltales that knowledge is our ruin; the knowledge of how naked and stupid we are. Well, if knowledge really is the only thing keeping us from living happy, naked lives, then here is something to chew on: knowledge is bad. Just knowing that knowledge is responsible for all the worst things I can think of makes me feel all sick and angry and perverted inside. Nevertheless, I am willing to go out on a limb and say that knowledge is not all it's cracked up to be, even if just because I am seriously that pissed at our public school system.

Don't get me wrong, public education is a good idea on paper. It's like a babysitter the government hires to discipline our children in a detention facility up to 90 minutes away from home by bus.[1] Yes, they don't really teach our kids anything other than how to pass standardized tests designed to make their school district look underfunded--yeah, that's what they do... the sick bastards--but consider the alternative! Debt, unemployment, an inaccessible job market: these are all facts of life that kids are supposed to go to grad school to find out. Public schools exist to take the "child" out of "child endangerment," to keep us average, and to transform the miracle of humanity into a nice, little robot powered by

---

1 Leslie Williams Hale, "Parents complain some Lee school bus rides 90-plus minutes long," *Naplesnews.com*, January 9, 2010.

fear and obedience.

However, I ask that you remember what it once meant to be a child: to be young, free, and wide-eyed in the wider world around you. Remember what it was like to not even know what homework was; to be ignorant to partisan gridlock or conspiracy theories. Remember your childhood, the good and the bad. Would you have traded it for anything? Of course not, and neither would I. These should be among the most precious moments of our lives. These were our moments when we did not know about war, tests, or standards. We were mutually ignorant to the world around us. This was our Paradise.

You remember these moments, and if you don't then they were probably driven out of you by a nanny hired by the state to whip you out of childhood until your innocence was lost. I speak of the kind of people who chide children for looking out a window instead of within the pages of a dead, lifeless book. Do any of you have the courage to deny a child the beauty of life, to pull a babe from his mother's breast, or to pluck a child from the embrace of summer's wane? I sure as hell don't, but that is what our schools are doing every day. They are not offering children a choice between their childhood and knowledge; they are forcing it upon them. What can a person learn about law after spending their entire youth incarcerated? How is a child supposed to sit straight if her chair has those annoying metal prods poking into her back? How the fuck is tubby supposed to learn how to read if you give him books that none of us would touch even if just to throw out? How are they supposed to live an independent life if the first lesson we teach children is that life is without choice?

I personally think a child has more to learn by staring at the stars at night than by staying up all evening doing homework. I believe a kid has the right to dream to his or her heart's content before being pulled out of Morpheus' arms by an alarm at the ass crack of dawn. I see no substitute for the parent no matter how much our schools pretend. I see no better motivator for a child than their own imagination. I take my own childhood as something so precious that if the state was to take one minute more of it from me they would have to fight me for it.

Think about it: why force a poet or an artist to sprint the shuttle run? Why insist that a chemist learn how to sew some underpants? Why turn something as supposedly useful as knowledge into something so repellent that it makes a child long for an escape? If anything, knowledge should be their vacation from the education life has to offer! Our own natural interests guide us in a manner as true for us as it was for our ancestors, but such interests should be fostered, not forced.

Even if a child is being raised in an environment that teaches him nothing but to enjoy life and love nature, he will be hunted down if he is not given an education that the state approves of. Families can be broken up, children sent to new homes, and parents branded as enemies of a state they had no choice being born into. How is that fair? How is that progress? How is that wisdom? I tell you it is none of these. How can something as intricate as the human mind be reduced to a scrap of paper that will dictate a person's life based on how they move their #2 pencil? This is not life, and this is not a childhood. If anything, it is an education in how to live our whole lives as robots. Dehumanization, indoctrination, and fear: these are the pillars of our education under the nanny state's care.

Such is what 'knowledge' has done to so many children: it destroyed the heaven that was rightfully theirs. Our schools have become a malicious experiment that no child should have to be forced into; a callous barter over our childhood by the state. As important as knowledge may be, it is nothing I am willing to massacre innocence over. It is something that I would gladly encourage, but never force.

It was a fine Paradise, this childhood, until knowledge destroyed it.

II

"Sleep is for the weak."
– Lord Harry Harry Hypnos

Hardly. Contrary to what you may have been unsuccessfully motivated with, sleep is also pretty important for the living last time I checked.

Sleep is a natural elixir; the chocolate mint on nature's pillow. If a fever was all Hippocrates needed to cure anything, a good night's sleep was his lollipop. Sleep is so important that it is both the first and last thing we do every day… or at least it ought to be. I don't know about you, but I plan on doing most of my dying when I'm dead. Sleep is for the living, not the weak or dying. With this in mind, why is it that so many of our teenagers--by which I mean all of them--look like they're zombies? Well, the talking heads will tell you that they are not getting enough sleep, but exhaustion is merely a symptom of an even worse pandemic which I call studentitis. It typically strikes every student from 5th grade to graduate school, and no, it is not typically found in nature. There are too many reasons to list why our students are not getting enough sleep, save one cardinal cause: our governments force them not to.

Sleep is no snake oil; it is a life-giving gift. It allows the body to recharge and repair itself, literally saving our lives every day. It lifts our spirits, takes us to strange, new places, and for some lucky dreamers it has made them world famous. However, there are more practical uses for sleep: it keeps us sane, fights off obesity, helps us process our memory, and helps us focus during the course of our day. In short, sleep actually makes us better students. You heard it here first, folks: Getting a full night's sleep is better for your brain than doing homework... or at the very least after a certain hour.

With this in mind, why is it that our schools find it necessary to keep their students so sleep-deprived with early-morning classes, fickle bus schedules, after-school activities, sports practice, and homework? These are children and adolescents we are talking about here, not adults.[2] There is no reason why our government should be forcing children throughout the nation to wake the hell up before their freaking parents. This is not a simple matter of fighting authority; these kids need these hours to grow. Just think about how many hours of your adolescence you lost to school when you should have been sleeping: Weeks? Months? Probably enough time to cost you a few inches of your height. I don't give a damn what they propagate about knowledge being power. Power is only as strong as the hand that wields it, and raising an entire nation of red-eyed students is no way to keep strong. Their overwrought workload is literally smothering them in their sleep, making us weaker and weaker as a population with each passing day. There is absolutely no way this war of attrition against our bodies can be rationalized. There is only one who stands to benefit from this standard, and it is... you guessed it, the goddamned state.

How sleep deprived are our young? Let me put it this way: when was the last time you heard of a student not falling asleep in class? Have you ever heard of anybody looking forward to getting up before sunrise? Has a

---

2 Yes, I know you kids don't like being called kids, but bear with me. I am trying to help you out.

medical journal ever recommended sitting down for eight to ten hours a day? Has anyone ever described spending a year in a public school as the foundation of good health? Have you ever looked forward to anything after a busy day--assuming it is not battery-powered--more than a nice, non-drug induced sleep? How about after a busy week, or a busy year, or a busy adolescence? For the love of God, what are they doing to us… Forcing any young adult to do anything in exchange for their rest makes as much sense as drinking your own blood for survival. It is as unsustainable as it is deadly.

The truth is that there is no time more important in a person's life to sleep than when they are young. Babies spend more than half their day sleeping, no exceptions. Children all the way up to preschool: 11-13 hours of sleep a day. Once they enter adolescence, on the other hand, that's where we see a serious sleep debt amounting. In the real world, your average teenager conservatively needs just as much sleep as your typical kindergartener: nine hours or more. For a high school student, getting nine hours of sleep is about as easy as running a four-minute mile. Sleep should not be fit into a teenager's schedule; it should own their schedule. Instead, the entire foundation for their health is being built on feet of clay.

How can anybody look into the tired eyes of a middle-schooler and see progress? How can anyone picture public school students as a school of fish swimming in an ocean of good health? How can any investment into our children's future be considered money well spent if it was done at the expense of their health? It is not, and it must be stopped. We need to cut our losses.

Your parents and your grandparents were pushed through the same tax-powered meat grinder that you are an unfortunate victim of as well. The toll this took on their minds and bodies--and on yours--is your legacy. The sins of the public school schedule are literally in your genes. It has slowly been killing you since before you were born, and it is too late to turn back the clock.

None of you are safe.

III

"Public funding for private schools is a match made in Heaven."
– Pope Nicholas III

I beg to differ.

First and foremost, let's make it clear that I am what you call an unlikely authority on private schools: Name a top school in the country, and there is a good chance I have been kicked out of it. I know academies that are famous for the sluttiness of their students. I know valedictorians who graduated more stoned than Stonehenge. I know a legendary dormitory so regularly flooded with booze that a friend of mine puked just from its smell. I have seen upper class orgies that consisted of more STDs than people. I have walked down the hallways of all-girl schools that were lined with dildos. To all you Lords and Ladies out there, to all you "elite," take it from me: your children are sick and twisted animals just like the rest of us mere mortals.

There, I said it.

Okay, so school vouchers... Where do I begin? If you go miniature golfing, do you pay for a driver as well as a putter? If you buy a gallon of nice, whole, hormone-laden milk, do you have to pay for 2%, 1%, or skim milk as well? If your pimpmobile runs on premium, do you also have to pay for regular and super? Hell no. In a free market world, you only pay for what you want! So, why in the world should it be any business of the state where family so-and-so sends their kids: public school or private? Well, for two reasons. One: they are paying for both. Two: depending on where you live, you might be as well.

The very idea of private schooling is all the evidence you need that public schools will have problems no matter how much money you pump in them. All the same, I am not much of a fan of private schools either. All 'elite' and 'fancy'... what are they hiding? All the uniforms in the world won't change the teenager underneath; the longer the sleeves, the more extensive the tattooing. Humans are driven by the same passions, hungers, and desires as they have been since the dawn of time, and nothing will change that. Even something as bland as a plaid skirt with suspenders will be made into a fetish, and has. Private school... please. If education in exile is such a benefit to the community/faith/agenda, why the hell charge people for it? They are already paying for public schooling, are they not? Not everybody has the luxury to pay for something as free as education twice.

Ah, but that is where the nanny state comes in. Even after she forced you to put your money into the public school system you despise, with one wave of her magic ruler she will provide you with a voucher for public schooling... which, incidentally, you paid for as well. Yes, you still have to be judged like a piece of meat to see if you, well, meet their standards, but even preferences over race, religion, weight, and other stupidities can be skirted for the sake of the almighty dollar. Unfortunately, this hits impoverished families unfairly hard; hence the public vouchers. Yup, that's what they tell you. Sure enough, there's a catch to it.

Public vouchers for private schooling may sound like a good idea on paper--unless you're smart like me--but the truth is that the public voucher system is so faulty it never even had the chance to fail. School vouchers are supposed to provide parents with the extra money they need to send their kids to private school even though they already paid for their public schooling like the good tax-payers they are. The voucher is supposed to make the added financial burden of private schooling easier, but what proponents of this policy fail to tell you is that they tend to benefit families who can afford to float the rest of the bill as opposed to families who can afford none of it. It's like being given a coupon to buy a castle: odds are the people who needed it most cannot afford to save the money.

Furthermore, this all assumes that young so-and-so was able to get a good-enough education at Demilitarized Zone Elementary to be a competitive applicant in the first place. Whose fault is it that a child is not able to meet admission standards: his biology, or the school that the fucking Fates provided him with? Public schools are public property, and if they are failing one student, then they are failing us all. We paid for them, and we have every right to see our investments get the attention they deserve. Instead of helping the well-off shop for private schools with tax-payer dollars, I suggest we put out the fires plaguing our public schools first.

IV

"We will feed your children with some decent food for thought."
– Ebenezer Cancercane, MP, Esquire

Likewise, out of all the transgressions the nanny state commits against us as students, few are viler, more distasteful, or more difficult to digest than the slop she serves us for lunch. For all our advances in agriculture, wealth, and technology, school lunches have become more unpleasant and less healthy than at any time since the invention of scrapple. While some might condemn the food industry for this conundrum, it is the state that contracts them with taxpayer money and keeps them in business. It is the state that opens their doors to their wares, and the state that encroaches onto what our children put into their mouths. With our nation and other nations facing an obesity crisis, it has never been more obvious just how foolish our schools' ventures into food retail have been.

Consider what the first students in our first public schools ate: an apple, some goat's milk, or maybe a rice cake? 2,000 years later such simplicities are now considered a luxury thanks to the corruption of our school system by corporate propaganda. Our own public schools, the very fruits of our public investments, have been made into servants of some of the largest companies on the planet. They pollute our halls of learning and health with candies and sodas, and serve as temptations for children no less disastrous for their health than a pervert with a lollipop. It has corrupted our children's growth, turned them into unhealthy adults, and caused a domino effect of consequences to fall on their future which just makes the state larger, more powerful, more expensive, and less effective.

It is any surprise that this has forced our government to spend billions of dollars to confront a global obesity crisis? These are dollars and Euros that could be used for more teachers, better textbooks, or... dare we say it... money that could have never left our pockets in the first place. Our northern neighbors have no national school meal program, and they are so healthy it almost makes you sick to think about it. School meals are simply a failed theory designed to empower the state to do what is essentially a parent's job: keep their children fed. Anything short of this should be considered cruelty. However, should a state force a child to eat a school lunch when something from home and possibly at home would be a better alternative, then I shall call cruelty in that case as well. Hell, maybe school should not even extend into the lunch hour in the first place.

Now, before you call me "Milk Snatcher," I ask that you chill the fuck out for a second. I am no bully; I simply look out for the children around me no differently than I would my own little brother. These are strange times we live in, and when our state is literally telling our students what to eat and when to eat it I cannot help but wonder what consequences this will have on their bodies until the day they die. Our natural resources have become more unnatural than ever; cow's milk has become such a volatile cocktail that even babies are beginning to grow breasts.[3] Overcrowding has forced students to literally revolve their eating schedules around how many students the state

---

3 "Chinese Parents Say Formula Grows Baby Breasts," CBS News, August 10, 2010.

can pack into a cafeteria at a time. Children are forced to eat foods they don't like and drink cheap, watered-down beverages. Am I crazy for saying 'What the fuck?' to a situation like this? I think not. If you want a madman, speak to whoever had the brilliant idea of adding foot-long hot dogs and Philly cheesesteaks to the cafeteria menu while trying to pass school lunches off as healthy.

Anything unhealthy for a child has no place in a school, especially since public schools are public property. Kids can't bring drugs, knives, or howitzers to class, so then why the hell do we allow peddlers to corrode our students' bodies with this garbage? I want cafeterias that serve nothing but fruit and vegetables grown on school grounds, unprocessed milk and yogurt supplied by local farms and nonprofits, healthy desserts whipped up during Chemistry, and maybe some wild boar hunted by the students as part of gym class. Not only would the obesity crisis in our country literally be cured, but our kids would be getting some decent exercise as well.

Ultimately, our school systems have been allowed to expand into something larger and more bizarre than a mere place for learning. They have become factories designed to serve as a surrogate for parenting, and they are just as bad at feeding children as they are at sending them to bed at decent hours. Schools will never be a substitute for parents and should not pretend to be. On the contrary, school is probably the single worst thing for the health of a child. For this reason, I suggest that parents take control of the situation before their children explode into something larger than the livestock our schools serve them.

I mean, how hard can it be to teach a kid how to pack a freaking lunch that won't kill them?

V

"When a teacher fails a student they are also failing their school, their country, and themselves as a teacher."
– Lord Oliver Cherkov

Every day our schools grow larger and more powerful while our teachers paradoxically seem to grow weaker. Teaching is something so precious to me that I would need to break both my hands to type it out for you. Teaching is the keystone in the archway of life; the central figure to any kind of personal development. These are people who are clearly not in their line of work for the money, for the hours, or for how good it is to their health. They are the citizen soldiers in humanity's war for survival and the leaders that we owe our entire future to, yet they are the ones who suffer the longest and hardest from the nanny state's failures at educating.

There are too many parents who like to blame teachers for their children's mistakes, but the reality is that these are the type of people who are fucking up the world by reproducing. The true purpose of a teacher is to make him or herself obsolete; to work towards a world that no longer needs their tutelage. This is an impossible enough job to attempt, never mind while having to deal with parents who are an even bigger handful than their children. So please, I ask that if you ever had a problem with your kid, consider the root of their problem: the one that extends into your own family tree. Don't blame rap, TV, your fears or your neighbors. I do not know a single world war or genocide that was instigated by lyrics or music video awards. All the more, while I do not believe in eugenics or sterilization, I will say that any parent who blames a teacher for their own failings should be personally punched in their reproductive organs by me. This, my vile nanny state, is something I am actually offering to do. For once, let's build toward something. Let me do this!

Don't get me wrong, there are some teachers who screw up and when they do they should be suitably dealt with due to the severity of their offenses, not based on how sexy they are. You know what I am talking about... When a guy gets a little too personal with one of his students, the courts sentence him to be anally raped in prison.[4] However, when a smoking-hot blonde fucks a dozen teenagers a few hundred times, she becomes lionized. I won't lie to you; as a teenager you bet your ass I wanted to get with some of my teachers. I spent more time studying Ms. Tingle's ass than any other subject from middle school to graduation. And you know why? Because that is what we teenagers are programmed to do. When humans reach sexual maturity, we want to get laid. Tragically, I never got with any of my hottest teachers--despite my advances--and that is what makes me all the more pissed when I hear about some jackass who scores with some fucked up whore a million miles out of his league. Nobody deserves that kind of special treatment in school, be they student or teacher, male or female, slamming or fugly. For the sake of justice, my dear judges, I ask that you be fair and consistent. Keep our laws standard for all adults. I am sick and tired of seeing a pervert paraded on television simply because of her sensational sex appeal.

So, let us use our imagination for a minute: There is progress! Parents are putting their full faith in their

---

4 Prisoners have a special system for this. I conducted interviews.

teachers, our teachers are doing exactly as they're told, and all these celebrity pederasts are a thing of the past. So, what exactly are these teachers instructing our students to do? How to build their own home? How to handle a crisis? Or better yet... how to teach themselves just about any subject on the planet? No. All students are learning is how to jump through hoops, perform tricks, and essentially behave little differently than any pet, beast of burden, or circus animal. What are they teaching us? How to take tests. Seriously, that's the sole function of the entire public school system. They're not teaching our children how to understand their material, how to use it in the real world, or how to remember it just a few months after graduation. All they are doing is forcing a child to behave like a robot that can fill in circles to a satisfactory level. This is not progress; this is a bestial form of conditioning that breaks down the human being into a soulless machine. It is a perversion of knowledge, and an education in dehumanization. All the more sorry, the school systems are not even very good at this job either.

The reason why this form of education is such an abomination is that it forfeits the very idea of learning for the sake of an individual school district's success. Teachers and students have in essence become pawns in a larger contest between other similar, sinister school districts for funding. They always want more money: More salaries, more reputation, and more laurels even though whenever they are given they are very rarely shared with the teachers who deserve them. That is what teaching has become, a game played by the most elite in the education business. It has been relegated to little more than a gamble over countless tax-dollars using our children's futures as chips. In such a state, it is any surprise that so many students graduate high school unprepared for what awaits them in college?

Naturally, these are all traits that are virtually impossible for the government to gauge, which is why the state keeps its teachers under such a tight grip. The state is afraid to let teachers do what they do best and be the inspirational individuals they truly are. The state won't let teachers think for themselves, obey their own wisdom, or exercise the full extent of their creativity in the classroom. As such, our school systems have become an enormous shackle designed to keep our teachers powerless, obedient, and as devoid of independent thought as the ideal student.

VI

"You can't beat the system, but the system can beat you."
– Lord Menelaus Draco

Good for you, system. Way to ruin our kids' lives.

I'm not going to pull any punches with standardized testing because standardized testing does not pull any punches with us. Standardized testing is a tool that has been turned into a torture device like the tanner's knife or ball gag. It is a theory that has become the judge, jury, and executioner for too many of our futures. It is a failed experiment, and one that should be taken no more seriously than astrology or alchemy. It is more feared than it could ever possibly be loved. It has shattered dreams and dashed hopes. It has destroyed more than it could have ever possibly built. Fuck it. Damn it. Let it burn. You hear me, you presumptuous bastard? I'm talking to you! Get over here, you lifeless little piece of paper! I want to spell this out for you right onto your fucking forehead!

F-U-C-K-Y-O-U

You know who you are, you standardized test, and I wrote that in a #2 pencil so that even you could read it, you illiterate, illegitimate, insidious, incestuous, insignificant, insipid, ignoble, illicit, irritating, idiotic, inappropriate, impudent, indignant, inept, inane, inimical, ineffable, indolent, infamous, inexorable, iniquitous, iconoclastic, ignominious, internecine, incubus-succubus, douchebag-asshole. You, my loveless standardized test, have become the antichrist of education and the antonym of wisdom. Oh, what a fool you've been, and what a fool we've been for fearing you.

But fear not, my dear readers. I know how to conquer this menace. I have seen the enemy, and there is none. Standardized tests are to schools what shit is to a bull.

Not too long ago, I was in Moscow with a friend of mine engaging in an exercise for the mind that I highly recommend. It's called travel. As we made our way toward Red Square we came across a haggle of vendors[5] who were peddling various wares with a cool, quiet dignity that anyone would be proud of. They offered everything from postcards to porcelain figurines when one vender selling Russian hats caught my attention. He was a cheerful man not much older than I who--as you could tell just from his face--was a student of the real world. Since I had already purchased a fine hat the day before for my father, I knew all too well that the hats this vendor offered were cheap knock-offs. However, that was exactly what I was there for: something cheap, terrible, and so hilariously out of date that it would instantly transport you to the '80s.

I picked up a jet black ushanka with such a proud hammer and sickle so proud that I imagined it would not even let snow obscure it. It was perfect! "How much for this?" I asked the vendor.

"16 rubles," he said. This magnificent gag-gift was for sale for less than the cost of a stamp.

"Wow, that is cheap," I nodded.

"Yes, it is cheap!" he added. "Eh... so cheap that if it breaks you don't care, 'cause it was so cheap."

We exchanged a glance that seemed to stretch an hour on that remark. At that moment, I knew I was standing face-to-face with the single greatest salesman on Earth. We both knew that he was selling a piece of

---

5 That's the proper term. Look it up.

junk, and we both knew that it was clearly not a refundable item. Nevertheless, his honesty coupled with the spreading grin on his face was all he needed to close the sale. I was completely won over.

"Brilliant!" I cheered. "I'll take two!" If I had enough heads, I would have purchased every hat in the shop.

I wish I could see this man again, but I know in my heart that I probably could not if I tried. He was honest, fair, generous, creative, adaptive, responsive, nonjudgmental, multilingual, ironic, witty, self-deprecating, self-employed, self-aware, and even selfless. He was all these qualities and a vendor selling imitation hats for less than 50 cents each, but my God... he was the king of his trade. Yet for all his talent, charm, brilliance, and life-experience there is not a single gift to his art that could be measured by standardized testing.

This, my dear reader, is why standardized testing must not stand and why we should not stand for standardized testing. It is not an adversary or an enemy; it is a big, fat nothing. It is a masterpiece of deception, pretense, and fear that fails at the very standard it sets itself to. It is not indicative of wisdom, virtue, art, nor conducive to imagination or creativity. On the contrary, all it does is punish the most innocent population on Earth for the failures of the state's own school systems. Big Sister had all the time in the world to prepare our students for anything, yet failed to prepare them for their own education. Had the state simply been honest about how important these tests would be taken, they would have drilled us in analogies and math problems from the moment we were old enough to distinguish calculators from boobs.

We already know the schools are not equal, so why force our students to shoulder the burden of the system's own failures? In one state a child learns about a Founding Father who is expunged from the history books just one school district over.[6] In one home a child is given tutors, study-guides, and even medication to aid in their test-taking abilities while in another a child is too overwhelmed with afterschool sports, clubs, and jobs to even put up a fair fight for their future. Our system tests us like cattle in the most uncomfortable chairs possible, smacks us upside the head with mind-numbing reading passages, and unsuccessfully dazzles us with math problems about as exciting as sex without foreplay. It is seriously like they are trying to test us in the most boring environment possible... which, interestingly, exists only when someone is taking a standardized test. This unfair, unnerving, unloving, unkind machine forces us to confine to its standards or else live in a world with more doors closed than open. It can truly be said that this machine has enslaved its maker.

I know virtuoso musicians who could not break 1000 on the SATs. I know valedictorians who crashed and burned the minute you took them away from their parents. I have shared tears with teenagers who lost their entire futures to analogies, had colleges reject them because of critical readings about fungi, and have stood beside parents as they unfairly buried their dead due to the suicidal stress of their studies.[7] I have seen my own academic successes treated with contempt and even sabotage by my peers, and have seen members of my own family denied awards because

---

6 James C. McKinley Jr., "Texas Conservatives Win Curriculum Change," *New York Times*, March 12, 2010.
7 According to the Centers for Disease Control and Prevention, "suicide accounts for 12.2% of all deaths annually" for 15- to 24-year olds.

of suspicions surrounding their own, honest ability. And lastly, I have seen the most academically successful students in my state prostitute their test-taking abilities to the most desperate students. I have suffered through their pathetic attempts to justify their actions in words that would hardly qualify for a 200 Verbal score. "It could make or break a scholarship," one of them told me as he assumed someone else's identity, and beat the system for him for a three-figure fee.

Such are the corrupt standards our system holds itself to, and such is the depressing desperation all of our students are facing.

VII

"Come now... Getting into a good school can't be all that difficult."
– Dean John Johnson, St. Johnson's University

Go sell your bullshit someplace else.

To you, my maladjusted public school system, I must ask what exactly you do for society. Are you here to provide us with the tools we need to survive? Hardly. The world needs more plumbers than lawyers at the moment, and package delivery men are slowly becoming the new doctors. Are these people failures for going to vocational schools or for simply avoiding college altogether? Have they let themselves down? In all honesty, I don't know. All I know is it is hard to find a package delivery man who is living in poverty. Impoverished philosophy majors, however... That is a different tale altogether.

Are you here to teach us how to follow our dreams? Tell that to the student whose graduate thesis was stolen; the athlete who lost his scholarship to a steroid-fueled meathead; the valedictorian rejected by every school she applied for; the foreign language expert forced to find work as a stripper; the graduate student who has been unemployed for a year; the homeless Ph.D; the jobless whistleblower; the teacher-bartender, or the vast, vast number of students who went to college just to major in debt. We are students. We are many. We are real. Tell me, my dear public schools, did you prepare us for that?

Did you warn us about the challenges we would face in all the wrong parts of the world? The parts where things are not as they should be? The corrupt, the nepotistic, the sexist, the racist, the envious, the arrogant, the narcissistic, the plutocratic, the oligarchic, the immoral, the amoral, the impassable, the insufferable, or the cruel? The parts everywhere, particularly here? Oh, no you didn't. You failed to provide us with the information, preparation, or the honesty we needed to survive this great struggle truthfully, respectfully, and fearlessly. We would not have blushed if you told us that not all authority can be trusted. We would not have shied away from our community if you had simply shown us how essential extracurricular activities were to admissions. It would not have hurt our feelings if you simply punched us just to teach us how to roll with them when they come. Why couldn't you give us what you always felt you were lacking at our age? Why couldn't you treat us like the adults we are, or you were! If to be adult is to be like you, well… fuck you!

Oh, education, how I weep for you. You were once a haven of enlightenment and a fountainhead of inspiration, but the sanctuary of your temples have long since been violated. You have allowed humanity's desperation for survival corrupt your interior, and make you larger, more cumbersome, and less efficient than ever. You have allowed yourself to be misled by too many cooks who don't know a whole lot about cooking. You have allowed something as precious as the future of your children to become just another political talking-point when it is really a non-issue. You have allowed students to be bullied, insulted, misled, and even killed in our schools' hallowed grounds because you refuse to admit when you're beat; when you don't know how to think like us, be there for us, or admit that you're wrong for our sake.

You are a victim, and so are your students. That is why I write this for you right now: for your funeral. You have become fearful, irresolute, and ignorant to the world around you, and the seeds of your failure have polluted every institution up to the Ivy League with your weeds. We are on the verge of an enormous bubble bursting, and its name is Education.

A curse on the people responsible for your suffering.

Rhetoric

I

"They call us public servants for a reason, you know. We're not the ones in charge of this country. The public is."
— Lord Monopoly Fisk

Easy for you to say.

What do most kids want to be when they grow up? A king, a queen, a princess, a pirate, a fairy, a firefighter, a cowboy, a president? I personally have no problem with this, and neither should you nor your parents. Sixty years ago an entire generation of cute little boys and girls grew up with the same hopes and dreams, but then something strange happened: they became politicians instead.

Seriously, how did this happen?

Don't get me wrong, there are some pretty good leaders out there. Corso Donati, for example, is a man of great principle. However, I think every single one of you knows who I am talking about when I voice my disgust with the mob that has made an entire career out of stealing, smearing, and shitting. I mean, who the hell wanted to be an asshole when they grew up? What kind of a kid actually dreams of becoming a charlatan; a bully; a lying bastard; a mudslinger; a carpetbagger; a snollygoster; a reactionary; a dogmatist; an obstructionist; the architect of a character assassination; a whore for the pharmaceutical industry; a whore to the oil industry; a whore for the abstinence industry; a whore to the military industrial complex; a whore to the environmentalist industrial complex; a warmonger; a peacemonger; someone who sleeps for only four hours a day; someone who likes to fool around with male pages; or nothing short of a goddamn pox of a person?

How did the public servant turn into a politician? It just does not make any sense. Public servants are supposed to be people we like! Not only that, we own them. In theory, these people are supposed to be in our pocket. We are supposed to be doing all the hiring and the firing. We are their highest authority. We are their master! So... what the hell happened? How did the politician usurp the throne of our chosen? Who are these people? Where did they come from? Why did they take over? Who died and made them boss! Ah, but therein lies the problem: the public servant died, and we are partially to blame.

We are the ones who allowed these insidious buggers to descend upon us like the swarm of locus they are. We looked the other way when they robbed us of our vote and were seduced by the luxury of self-preservation to sit out the fight for the fate of our country. However, we are talking about bigger and even fouler fish than someone who simply sleazed into office, played off the politics of fear, prejudice, hate, or simply had a friend or family member steal the election. There is something sinister afoot even more irritating than the post-primary phone call: I speak of the spoils system; the downward-drip of corruption; and the understandable corrosion of faith in our government. Public service is no longer a duty; it is a trade that has become more overreaching and more consequential for more people with time. The responsibility was never supposed to be about moneymaking, but for some it has become an even bigger business than sex.

Now, I am not suggesting that we simply do away with government. On the contrary, I think anybody dumb enough to support anarchy should be kicked swiftly and repeatedly in the ass. Community is necessary for civilization to endure, but that should in no way suggest that any government is better than no government at all. Our particular government has been infiltrated by villains who have transformed it into a machine dedicated to their own self-preservation. These people, for the sake of discussion, I call the nonpublic servant. They know and obey only their sources of power, and have built entire careers off of perverting their office. Public service is merely a prescription that these nonpublic servants abuse like a drug, and believe me when I say this: it has become their addiction. True public servants, the Mr. and Mrs. Smith's of the world, have unfortunately become an endangered species. The seats of these good men and women have been usurped by a desperate, insatiable cabal, a cabal that figured politics was their best weapon in their own personal fight for survival.

The only question that remains about these nonpublic servants is who the hell it is they are serving. Is it a shadow government? A vast conspiracy? I find that doubtful. Their master is their own mortality, and they will do anything to fend it off.

It is for this reason that you would be hard-pressed to find a self-dubbed conservative who actually makes our government smaller. They need a big government to make their new own new order happen, and it is unlikely that they would ever relinquish this power. It would put them out of their own jobs.

II

"Down with big government!"
—Some genius who voted to spend $1 trillion on a land
war in Asia.

Quit ruining whatever civil discourse is left in society with your stupidity.

Before we give the political machine behind the nanny state the rhetorical dropkick it deserves, it would be unfair for us to ignore the hypocrisy on parade by its so-called opponents. Too many politicians, pundits, and would-be experts have made infuriatingly lucrative careers portraying themselves as heroes to the common asshole in their crusade against big government. They have rallied radicals to their cause--both religious and the just plain crazy kind--deployed every logical fallacy in the book to mislead voters, published countless books that read like they were written by the same douchebag, and have already stalled their way into the history books. These people are the opposition party--our best, last defense against the nanny state. These are our vanguards.

Dear reader, do not be fooled by these false prophets.

It should go without saying that anyone who turns money in the bank into money in the hole should not be considered fiscally conservative, but that is for another chapter. For right now, let's just talk about what our would-be heroes have done to keep us safe from the nanny state. You know, like shrinking the size of government, cracking down on reckless spending, eliminating wasteful infrastructure, not even thinking about touching our individual rights, and--

for fuck's sake--remaining cool with our neighbors. That's not too much to ask, is it? Asking for less? Who wouldn't want a slimmer, sexier government with better mileage, smoother handling, and none of that "malaise" bullshit? With that as our platform, how could our vanguard possibly fail!

Oh, but fail they did, and these bastards failed us royally, morally, ethically, epically, confoundedly, compoundedly, unjustifiably and irreconcilably bad!
That's right. The very people who you conservatives out there thought would keep you safe from big government not only did jack shit to rein it in, they actually made it larger: They added a multibillion-dollar department to our bureaucracy that has spent more than a quarter of a trillion dollars on such necessities for homeland security as "dog booties" and beer brewing kits.[8] They have invaded our privacy more than ever before with a freaky little law that pretty much gave the government unlimited power to spy on whoever the fuck they want. They subpoenaed a man and his bedridden, nonresponsive wife to testify about something that was clearly not the government's business: her death. They have declared war on the female reproductive system. They have made it illegal to look Mexican. They rewrote and subsequently broke the rules on torture. They nearly doubled the national debt. They tried to nationalize a language. Oh, and best of all, they called for, approved, and signed into law the largest bailout in recent history. Way to go, conservatives. Way to keep us safe from government.

Naturally, this is not even touching the crazier/stupider/more personally offensive subject regarding "the sanctity of marriage." I mean... For real? This is what our public

---

8 "Report: DHS employees wasted thousands," MSNBC.com, July 19, 2006.

servants are doing with themselves? Since when was it the government's business to intervene in religious disputes! It's bad enough that people need to apply for a license to get married as if spending the remainder of your life with someone is akin to going duck hunting. Until one of these religiously conservative/paranoid jackasses starts pushing for constitutional amendments outlawing adultery, shotgun weddings, or purchasing crystal meth from a 200 lb. male prostitute named Tiny, I will continue to call bullshit on this whole fucking debate. It's chicanery. It's jugglery. It's theater. It's designed to do nothing more than get the single most uncompromising voting bloc in the nation--religious radicals--in their corner. This is worse than a marriage between church and state: It is an adulteration between the public servant and the public who put them into office.

And don't even get me started on the war…

So, these are our champions in our war against the nanny state: a bunch of self-serving, two-faced assholes that would probably have our government outlaw everyone but themselves if they had the chance. Actually, scratch that… They can't put us all in chains because if they did there would seriously be nobody left for them to fuck. These people fucked their own country, fucked their own people, fucked their own cause straight in the ass, fucked their nation's financial future, fucked our reputation with our neighbors, and have made the nanny state into their mistress.

In fact, when you think about it, the only people they haven't fucked are their wives.

III

"Down with big government!"
– [same jackass]

"We don't have to debate about what we should think about
homosexual activity, it's written in the Bible....I think I know what you
did last night, if you send me a thousand dollars I won't tell your wife!"
—[Different jackass, only this one got busted buying
meth from a 200 lb. male prostitute]

Ugh...

Sorry to bring this up again, but I am still so fucking
pissed over these so-called enemies of nanny state who are
really just assholes in sheep's clothing.

As I write there is a conspiracy afoot in this great nation
of ours to make the government as large as possible by
those who claim to value "values." These so-called social
conservatives are in actuality fundamentalist radicals who
have declared a holy war against a planet they cannot
possibly convert. It is our nature as humans to evolve and
adapt--whether you accept it or not--for the benefit of
the species. Every generation in our history has enjoyed
more rights, liberties, and equality under our laws than
their forbearers. It is called progress, and anybody who has
a problem with that is welcome to bullshit all they want
about how insecure they are with the inevitability of the
future. We have the ability to ignore them, but I will not
lay flat on my belly as these snakes hijack our government
and pervert it into a trans-nanny state better known as a
theocratic tyranny.

Our government has no business whatsoever intervening

in religious affairs if for any other reason than because religion is a debate that cannot be won. There is no true faith just as there is no perfect government, and even if there were, we are too drunk and stupid to effectively organize it. Religion, like government, is flawed because it is a human institution. I am not claiming that I know all the answers, but I am positive that if there is one thing we can agree upon it is how freely the cup of human stupidity runneth over. No matter how good an idea is, be it the word of man or of God, there is no shortage of dicks, douchebags, or dumbasses on the planet to corrupt it with their own personal faults. If anything, faith should be something so precious to people that they would not even consider denigrating it to something as trite as a political point. That would be crass.

These social disputes are literally bleeding our country more and more with each passing debate. As of this hour, more than 13,000 men and women have been discharged from our military for no other reason than being who they are. Do you have any idea what a mammoth state is required to institute such a doctrine; that a person must have doors shut to them forever for no other reason than sexual orientation? Be it the product of homophobia or religious radicalism, such standards offer no product whatsoever for our nation. "Values" are not a product or a gain, and any investment in them can only result in a loss. It has not made us any safer, healthier, more tolerant, and its very aim is to empower the state to drive a wedge between rational debate and consensus-building. Religion is non-negotiable, uncompromising, and absolute. By trickling up into our government it has empowered the state to make us even worse off than if there was no state at all.[9]

---

9 Think about that for a minute... Okay, good.

Empowering the state to rule over a person based on their sexual orientation is a slippery slope of shit that everyone should avoid. I do not care how many "values" these paranoids tack onto it; an assault on the liberty of one is an assault on the liberty of us all. Should the government ban heterosexuals from serving in the military if they had experimented with homosexuality while in college? Or high school? Or middle school? Or while a child? What about someone who practices oral sex, or anal sex, or mammary intercourse, or has a boot/foot/pedal fetish? Or is bisexual, or asexual, or into something kinda cool but ultimately offensive to just one person who happens to own a megachurch, or a news corporation, or a politician? What business it is of theirs how somebody else gets off? For fuck's sake... how did we get here! Don't we have better things to do than obsess over other people's sexual orientation?

All the worse, what kind of precedent does such a standard create for the nanny state? Should law enforcers, firefighters, or rescue workers be subjected to the same homophobic standard? What about mail carriers, or morticians, or teachers?[10] Or how about anybody that is drawing a federal salary: senators, legislators, judges, assistants, secretaries, attorneys, or even presidents? Since the president is commander-in-chief of the military, does the status quo standard make it impossible for a homosexual to ascend to that position in this great nation of ours, even if by popular vote? Worse still, is it illegal simply to think homosexual thoughts without actually acting upon them? Could certain dreams cost a person his or her job? Could this apply to all tax-paying citizens as well? Or to our allies? Or to all the peoples of the world?

10 This goes for unmarried heterosexual sexually-active female teachers as well, according to the most prominent teabagger in Congress.

Jesus Christ... are we just the beginning?

Yes, slippery slopes are a logical fallacy, but does one need to speak logically to dismiss something that is illogical? Our vanguards for small government are hypocritical, homophobic bigots, and ultimately cowards too insecure about their own faith, social standards, and/or sexual orientation to see anything in the world that stands in contrast to it. Such lunatics would paint the world red if they could. Their problems are not our problems, and they are most certainly not our government's problems. However, you bet your ass they want to make their problems a state matter for us until Judgment Day.

IV

"Sex is a terrible, immoral, sinful act that has no place in a decent society. It should be bound, slapped, branded, handcuffed, tied down to a bed, flogged, spanked, teased, humiliated, sworn at, spit on, forced into obscene poses, unusual poses, and poses you would have never guessed possible unless someone took a picture of it. In short, sex is carnal, animalistic, and inhumane. In a perfect world we would all be celibate."

– Rev. Gaylord Savage

If you think religious radicals and social reactionaries can be placated in their crusade against gays, then I've got news for you: they want to declare war against all forms of sex. Homosexuals, heterosexuals, bisexuals, transsexuals, and now autosexuals--a supermajority of our nation--are under siege by a not-so-clandestine campaign to prohibit non-reproductive sex of all kinds. Its soldiers claim to be devotees of small government and free speech, but in actuality they are Christian fundamentalists bent on converting the nanny state into a totalitarian theocracy. They want to outlaw sex education[11], they want to outlaw abortion[12], they want to outlaw all forms of contraception[13], they want to outlaw dildos, vibrators, and other pleasurable products,[14] they want to outlaw breastfeeding in public[15], and, most recently, they want to be given the power--or at the very least the platform and the funding--to tackle what they consider to be one of the most rampant, widespread threats to our civilization: masturbation.[16]

That's right, masturbation.

11 Except abstinence, of course.
12 Even though it would be political suicide if they did.
13 Again, except abstinence.
14 They refer to them as "genital stimulating devices." Also, WTF?
15 Come on! That's not even sexual!
16   For real.

I mean, seriously... half the population has probably masturbated today, and the other half is probably masturbating right now. Masturbating is not a vice; it is a tool for survival. It's a skill passed on through evolution to, oh, I don't know... keep us from going insane. Hijacking the nanny state to outlaw pleasurable devices is one thing, but cracking down on the oldest discovery? That would create such a ridiculously large government that I am afraid just to joke about it.

In fact, I am not going to allow this debate to violate our privacy one second longer, even if just hypothetically. Life is too short to waste it on reasons why you should be able to masturbate. All I'll say is that if you can prevent people from doing something as natural as having sex with each other, you can probably make them do anything.

And, in all honesty, that is what makes the masturbation debate so fucking scary to me. These radicals are so lost that I do not even know who I am speaking to anymore.

V

"The only people concerned about personal privacy are
people with something to hide."
                                   – John Arschloch, J.D.

My ass!

Playing around with people's privacy is a very dangerous
game. In fact, I think the only thing I would compare it to
is Russian roulette. Privacy is one of the oldest rights we
have been entitled to since the invention of the cave--or,
lacking one, since our earliest ancestor first took a dump
behind a bush. It is also something very important to me
because I consider personal privacy to be personal property.
We all own our privacy just as much as we own our bodies,
and there is no way anybody can convince me that it can
be sacrificed for personal safety. Allowing the nanny state
to poke and prod at our most sensitive information is a
crime on its own that cannot be rectified or portrayed
as anything other than theft. Our privacy is ours, and
nobody can take it from us. It is a liberty as inalienable and
immutable as liberty itself. Similarly, liberty and privacy are
two inseparable rights that cannot be bartered with.

In short, I don't care what security you're selling, Nanny
State. Go mind your own business!

Part of the reason why I take personal privacy so
seriously is not because I have that many things to
hide. On the contrary, I see privacy as an escape from
criticism, persecution, and disagreement. In short, privacy
is humanity's best, last hope from fear. We all have dirty
laundry because being flawed is part of the miracle that is
humanity. The nanny state, however, believes in perfection.

It is willing to act on absolutes because it has been empowered to do so. The nanny state can track you down, kick down your door, defile everything you own, move you, imprison you, torture you, and execute you simply because of what it thinks you've done. It works in absolutes, which is terrifying because humanity is absolutely flawed. As long as there is one person in this great nation being profiled for no criminal wrongdoing whatsoever, all of our privacy is at risk, all our safety, and all our lives.

Oh, and the best part about all this unnecessary debate about surveillance: all its blowhard proponents who say that it exists to keep us safe from terror. Their preaching and pontificating is nothing short of an attempt to terrorize our entire population with their Christian fundamentalism. If you ask me, the state should start considering how to keep us safe from itself. The global war on terror will never be won nor effectively waged until it is eradicated from our homeland, and right now I think the biggest threat to homeland security is, in fact, our homeland security.

VI

"No law, nation, treaty, or person can stop us from torturing whomever we want, whenever we want, however we want. Sometimes you gotta break balls to make someone talk, even if they are the balls of some guy's kid. That's leadership."

– Bertran de Born

In all honesty, I wish I was making this stuff up, but a Roman Catholic who graduated summa cum laude from one of the top schools in the country, received his J.D. from another one of the best schools in the country, and, while serving as the deputy assistant attorney general to the Department of Justice, co-authored a series of documents unabashedly known as The Torture Memos was actually asked the following question:

> "If the President deems that he's got to torture somebody, including by crushing the testicles of the person's child, there is no law that can stop him?"

He answered:
> "No treaty."
> "Also no law by Congress -- that is what you wrote in the August 2002 memo..."
> "I think it depends on why the President thinks he needs to do that."[17]

Oh, and just to make sure that this legal expert/asshole was not completely stoned when he said that, Congress followed up on his statements a few years later:[18]

---

17 For the sake of anonymity, he will be referred to here as "Asshole."
18 U.S. Congress, House Subcommittee on the Constitution, Civil Rights, and Civil Liberties of the Committee of the Judiciary, *From the Department of Justice to Guantanamo Bay: Administration Lawyers and Administration Interrogation Rules (Part III)*, 110th Cong., 2nd sess., 2009, Committee Print.

Chairman: "It was reported that you were asked if a president could order a suspect's child be tortured in a gruesome fashion and you responded that "I think it depends on why the president thinks he needs to do that. Is that accurate?"

Asshole: "Mr. Chairman, I don't believe it's accurate because it took what I said out of context. (I see) The quote stopped right before I continued to explain the number of things which I appreciated the opportunity..."

Chairman: "So far what I read was accurate, but there was more?"

Asshole: "But it stops at mid sentence, I mean I finished the sentence during the debate but I didn't get a chance to..."

Chairman: "OK, thank you...Is there anything professor Asshole that the president cannot order to be done to a suspect if he believed it necessary for national defense?"

Asshole: "Ahhh, Mr. Chairman, I think it goes back to the quote you just read because..."

Chairman: "No, I'm just asking you the question, maybe it doesn't, but what do you think?"

Asshole: "I think it's the same question I was asked..."

Chairman: "Well, what's the answer?"

Asshole: "First, can I make clear I'm not talking about..."

Chairman: "You don't have to make anything clear. Just answer the question, Counsel."

Asshole: "I just want to make sure I'm not saying..."

Chairman: "You don't have to worry about not saying, just answer the question."

Asshole: "OK, my thinking right now?"

Chairman: "Yes, right now. This moment."

Asshole: "This moment...My thinking right now, first, the question you're proposing..."

Chairman: "WHAT is the answer?"

Asshole: "Mr. Chairman, I'm trying to make...."

Chairman: "No you're wasting my time....Look, Counsel, we've all practiced law..."

Asshole: "I don't think the President..."

Chairman: "Hold it. Could the President order a suspect buried alive?"

Asshole: "Mr. Chairman, I don't think that I have ever..."

Chairman: "I am asking you that."

Asshole: [continuing] "...Given the advice that the President could bury someone alive."

Chairman: "I didn't ask you if you ever gave him advice, I asked you do you think the President could order a suspect buried alive?"

Asshole: "Mr. Chairman, my view right now is I don't think a president would - no American president would ever have to order that or feel it necessary to order that."

Chairman: "I think we understand the games that are being played..."

Yes we do, Mr. Chairman. Yes we do indeed...

The last administration came into power with a pledge to reduce the size of government, stay out of nation-building, and ultimately put the nanny state out of everyone's misery. They had control of the presidency, the legislature, the courts, and nearly unanimous support to do whatever thanks to a sudden outflowing of patriotism. Our nation had been attacked, and our leaders had nearly unanimous support to do, literally, whatever they wanted to the country. This was the best, and perhaps the last opportunity to put our country so far backwards the nanny state would not even know what hit her.

Instead, eight years later we have learned the scary truth. Not only did they make our government bigger, they made it scary than ever before. With unbridled power to eavesdrop, imprison, torture, and even murder whoever they ominously considered "enemies," be they foreign or domestic, these champions for our cause had become werewolves in the night. Oh yes, we have seen this "New Day" they promised us, and it looked more like a worst-case scenario nanny state: a police state, a military-industrial state, a terror state.

Don't ever trust these lying bastards with our nation's car keys again. Fuck them.

VII

"The purpose of government is to make everyone equally unhappy."
– Joe the Political Scientist

Reader, we need to have a very serious discussion about the state of our country.

Ultimately, both the left and right wings of our two-party system are able to agree on one thing: they both want big government. The only difference is that the left wing wants there to be big government for the sake of equality--or at the very least equality for the oppressed and/or impoverished--while the right wants big government for a much more baffling reason.

Conservative political ideology cannot exist without embracing liberty and individualism as its core tenet. Where there once was a viable alternative to big government, that opposition has been commandeered by a coalition of religious and social fringe groups who are impossible to reason with. They will yield no quarter in their campaign to make our nation religiously and socially exclusive to their own antiquated, reactionary standards. They want us to hold the same values as them. They want us to worship and fear the same God as them. They want us to look like them, behave like them, and perhaps most importantly to do as they tell us. They require a larger government than the one we have now to make this possible, and that is why they can never be trusted with our state. They have made civil discourse impossible because they do not respect their opposition. They have gone mad with power because they want to rule us like Gods. They are so narcissistic that they believe only what they want to believe, even at the expense of whitewashing reality. These callous cranks are a cancer to conservative political ideology and to our country as a whole. They are not conservatives, and they never were. They are just assholes, bullies, and shouters. I never liked shouters.

So, where do those who want to stave off the nanny state go? I do not know, but I do know that the old guard has failed them. I would suggest that the nanny state simply be put out of business by offering an alternative that is more appealing in every way: a government that accomplishes more by doing less. In other words, a government that does only what the people need of it, not what they want of it. People need to play a larger role in their government by making it clear what they absolutely need it to do and what they need it to butt out of. Voting is optional, and I would never force the vote upon people. However, it is possible that through better leadership people would have a better understanding of their own personal duty to their country. This can only be accomplished if the public servant reclaims his seat from the politician.

One such public servant can be found in the annals of history to serve as a role model for future leaders to follow. He was a young boy who was tutored by his father on equanimity, justice, consensus-building, and respect. He was a child who was raised by his mother to be true to his family for the strength of them all. He was a young man who suffered greatly at the hands of bullies and antagonists, but who never forgot to repay a good deed. He was a devoted husband and family member who never let anything get between him and his kin. He was a brilliant political and military scientist who knew that strength was not in numbers, but in well-organized numbers. He was a man of absolute fairness and justice who wholeheartedly loved his people regardless of race, religion, gender, or class, and they all loved him back. Simply by leading his people through example, he was able to create the largest empire in history ruled by the smallest government possible. It was the largest empire ever created in the life of one man, and who would have thought… it was an empire of nomads.

His name was "Iron-worker," perhaps better known as Temüjin, and eventually better known as Genghis Khan. He killed tens of millions of people, erased entire nations off the map, and was not only a better defender of small government than these assholes we have now, but an easier one to get along with.

Yes, that's how bad the present opposition to the nanny state is. It makes me wish that Genghis Khan could somehow mount a political comeback.

Logic

I

"Public smoking should not be outlawed here or there; it should be outlawed everywhere."
– Lord Hyphen Butts

All right, I don't even know where to start with this one. It's like trying to find the best part of a shit sandwich to take a great big bite out of, or the preferred testicle to have chewed off by a Rottweiler. Or better yet, the best subject on which to waste every fucking second of your fucking life before you die. Public smoking...

While I am not a smoker myself aside from the occasional cigar, clove or fattie[19], I consider the hypocrisy of my outrage none the lesser of any non-smoker who considers himself or herself an expert on all things smokable. Smoking is not just a way of life; it is a way of death. It is how five million people from around the world choose to die every year[20], and you know what? Who are you to judge them! If time is spent like money, then aren't all ways of life nothing more than ways of death? Do the countless hours we spend working out in the gym keep us safe from car crashes or is that vegan bullshit people eat going to protect them from meteors? I think not. Life is a ticking time bomb that is just waiting to go off, and anybody who thinks they have the power to pry the cigarette from a smoker's blackened fingers has another thing coming their way.

Consider if you will the very idea of smoking bans: that the best way to keep non-smokers safe from cigarettes is to ban smoking in public places. Well, what about those of

---

19 Which are awesome.
20 Give or take.

us in ground zero: those of us who smoke? You know, all 1.1 billion[21] of us who bullshit through our jobs and pay our taxes like any other honest citizen. We have enough numbers to form our own religion yet are treated like a minority. Why should we have to take any bullshit from our governments when it comes to public smoking? If anything, our governments should be taking bullshit from us!

Take these stupid warning labels they put on cigarettes as if anyone who is old enough to buy them is going to take them seriously. "May cause birth defects,"

"This will kill you,"

"Seriously, you're going to die." Please... They could be playing The Passion of the Christ on these packages on an endless loop and people would still buy them until the day they die. Do you know why? Because we are fucking addicted to them. Seriously, it's like masturbation. Once you learn what nicotine feels like it becomes as important to you as jerking off in the shower. And you know what? We like it! Yeah, it is killing us, but what the hell is wrong with living your entire life while enjoying the best damn legal drug on the planet? I mean, the only reason why we're not all taking Soma is the simple fact that it doesn't exist. Instead of that wonder drug, we have cigarettes. You don't like that? Well, who cares. You? Haha! Yeah, that'll be the day... I don't even know you!

Mankind's addiction to ~~masturbation~~ cigarettes is the reason why you can charge so much for them without there being any shortage of demand. $2 a pack, $10 a pack... we don't care. We must have it. So, what is Big Sister's response to this? They jack up the taxes on cigarettes. Yes, they play the same role as a fat don eager to "wet their

---

21 The WHO. Don't believe me? Look it up yourself.

beak" off our addiction. I ask you right here and now: who is the real victim here? Is this how you rescue a person from addiction: by taking advantage of their handicap? If we truly are dying here, then you should be there to help us! If anything, the government should be paying us not to smoke.

If this all comes down to money, then why not just go after the kingpin? Tax the shit out of the tobacco industry and let the rest of us taxpayers affordably smoke in peace! They are the ones who got us hooked as kids. They are the ones who put all this crazy crap into our lungs and clothing. They are the ones who came up with the bizarre additives crammed into cigarettes instead of stuff that freshens our breath, whitens our teeth, or is loaded with Vitamin A. How come they didn't just slip nicotine in good things like toothpaste or mouthwash so that we could get our buzz from that? Oh, I don't know... eggplants? These are all questions your local parliamentarian should be sweating the tobacco companies over instead of average folks like you and me. We are all just innocent bystanders.

So, I tell you right now that smoking cigarettes in public is not our problem. The problem is that the cigarette companies have yet to invent a better cigarette. Don't treat us like we're assholes simply because we have a monkey on our back. Go for the head of the serpent instead of the dick of the donkey. Put down your picket signs and hold the feet of every tobacco company in the country to the fire until they invent a cigarette as good for you as salmon. We smokers really don't give a fuck. As long as we can still get a buzz from it, we'll be cool. All we want is for these non-smokers to get off our asses. However, knowing them, they are probably always going to find something to gripe over.

II

"Reducing the drinking age would harm society, legalizing marijuana would cripple it, and decriminalizing every other drug would effectively kill it."
— Rev. Gaylord Savage

On the contrary, I think the War on Drugs has become a sicker, deadlier, and even more addictive habit for our nation to kick than any other drug on the menu.

The very subject of criminalizing or not criminalizing drugs raises the question as to just how deep into our daily lives our governments should be prodding. In one culture every drug but cigarettes, alcohol, and prescription medicines are illegal. In another, all firearms save unlicensed weapons, automatics, and high-yield explosives. In another still all foods deemed "high" in sugars, fats, and cholesterols. What standards are they held to? What maxims do they obey? Proponents of such regulation claim that it is good for society, but if you ask me regulation is rotting us from the inside just like the cancer from our cigarettes.

First and foremost, all forms of social or moral regulation are relative. By jumping in on the social-vice bandwagon, our government, courts, and legal systems have essentially entered into a philosophical debate. This is a debate that they cannot possibly win for more than one reason, not the least because every single adult on the planet has gotten drunk or high at some point in their lives.[22] Secondly, it is a cause that is riddled with hypocrisy. How is one drug valued or appraised with respect to legality? One could argue that handguns should be outlawed, or gambling, or

_____
22 Ditto for Philosophy majors.

automobiles or even junk food based on the toll they take on society. If our government tried to criminalize deep-dish pizzas or online gaming with as much fervor as they have hounded drug dealers and seekers, do you think it would make any difference to people if you told them that both vices are just as addictive as heroin? Hell the fuck no! Addictive behavior comes in too many forms to be effectively prohibited in any way.

Secondly, the best way and safest way to take on drug cartels is to simply legalize their illegal product and put them out of business. If the government lifted the ban on all drugs from marijuana to coke, you know that our farmers would be ass-deep in the stuff. It is a commodity that can be commercialized, commoditized, flavored, and--from a government standpoint--taxed to no end. I mean, do you have any idea how much the entire drug industry would make if the government simply joined in on the action? We would be kings. Seriously, kings. Revenues on weed-sales alone could probably finance the entire federal government now that drug enforcement has been retired and prisons made less crowded. The entire national budget could be balanced based on the price of the weed and prices would still be too low for any drug dealers to compete. Furthermore, commercial airlines would probably experience a significant boost thanks to the inevitable sale of duty-free drugs while traveling. Hell, people might even be getting high in the sky at some point.

And lastly, drug dealing is simply too good an education in mathematics, accounting, social networking, entrepreneurship, scheduling, business, international relations, the metric system, vocabulary, debate, risk management, addictive behavior, and supply and demand economics for our publics schools to possibly compete with. The practice must be eliminated if we are to ever have our schools survive long enough to get their shit together.

Legalizing drugs offers nothing but benefits. Anyone who says otherwise is simply so dependant on denial that they can truly be called a denial-addict. Yes, addictive behavior should be discouraged just as it is with any other pleasure on the planet, but that is society's problem to solve and not the government's… and, most certainly, not the goddamned nanny state's. Our government's efforts to curb drug use, possession, and sale has only made us more expensive, less effective, and more hypocritical as law enforcers than when our predecessors [unsuccessfully] dabbled with Prohibition. There is nothing wrong with admitting that you are wrong about something, especially when it means money in your pocket and a healthy philosophical barometer.

Besides, if recreational drug use was truly as bad as they say for society, then why out of all the other places on Earth is the International Court of Justice housed in the Netherlands?

III

"I do not believe in the death penalty. However, I will
defend the death penalty to the death."
— Judge Santos

Presented for your consideration: the death penalty.

I sometimes ask myself whether the death penalty can
truly be justified as a mental exercise. Does it take a large
or a small government to kill a person? I would say that it
takes a larger government because you are essentially taking
away the most important thing in that person's life as far
as the state is concerned. To speak in support of the death
penalty is to advocate the arrest and the imprisonment
of someone, their trial, the debate over their verdict, and
eventually their termination at the hands of the state. This
is perhaps the largest thing a government can do: To take
or not to take the life of one of its own citizens.

I am not going to weigh the pros or cons of executing a
criminal with respect to the alternative of life imprisonment. I
will not tackle this from a moral, social, or religious perspective,
and do not even care what the courts of our country have
decided on the subject. I want to discuss this in full impartiality
and out of no love for humanity, so bear with me for a moment.
For the rest of this chapter, consider me to be inhumane.

Firstly, executing anybody for any reason is the kind of
thing that you gotta be pretty sure of yourself before you go
into it. Once you kill the person, there is no turning back.
If you fucked up for any reason, the person is dead. As we
have established previously, I have nothing but confidence
in the endless stupidity of humanity. Our nation can and
has executed what we now know to be innocent people.

They are too many for me to list; just know that they exist. While we could say that justice was delivered impartially and all proper procedures were followed, it does not change the fact that our government wasted the time and the money to take an innocent life. Also, you know, we wasted that life as well.

Until humanity irons out the defects of its own imperfection, I simply cannot support the continued operation of capital punishment. Humanity is flawed. Our systems of governments are flawed, our laws are flawed, religions are flawed, and you bet your ass our elected officials are flawed. Empowering them with enough trust to terminate a person's life if they feel it is necessary is nothing short of gullibility at best and criminal laziness at most. If just one out of the last hundred people we have executed were actually innocent, or out of the last thousand people we executed, or out of all the people we have executed in our history, I would say that our government is so callous, slothful, and narcissistic that it is willing to kill one innocent person for the sake of what they consider a functional system. Our courts will never function perfectly as long as we have humans running them, but while cases can be appealed and convictions overturned, there are no do-overs when it comes to capital punishment.

The nanny state has no right to tell certain people to stop appearing in public, to show up at a certain court again and again, to be tried, erroneously convicted, and eventually told that it would better off for society if they were quietly killed. Even if it happens once a year or every 100 years, it is still happening, and nobody deserves to live in a government so large that it considers killing an innocent person as an acceptable loss simply to preserve the delusion that our laws and our courts are as good as we would like.

They are not. Oh, dear reader... they are so not.

IV

"Legalize prostitution? You've got to be kidding me?"
– Rear Admiral Ramsbottom

Enough with the kidding, Ramsbottom, because the only person you are kidding is yourself.

A person's body is their own fucking business, and this is particularly true when it comes to the fucking business. Sex is a trade no different than any other form of hard labor. It is a skill no different than endurance tests or athletics. It is a talent and a form of expression no different than any other art form. It is a way of life, and a way of this world. It is a natural resource of humanity, and as such it is one that I believe our government should stop flipping the fuck out over.

To begin with, prostitution is called the oldest profession for a reason: it is the oldest profession. It enjoys a history even older than the Bible and a rich social legacy in art, music, theater, literature, and opera. It takes one hell of a nanny to grow britches big enough to deny a population something which has been part of our culture going back to the dawn of civilization, but that is exactly what is going on in our country. This is not out of peer-pressure; the majority of our allies in Europe enjoy legalized prostitution. Furthermore, it is not out of health or hygiene. The rate of HIV/AIDS for adults in our country is nearly twice that of the European community,[23] and STDs are exploding among teenagers with no thanks to prostitution being criminalized. In the end, it is outlawed simply because of religious standards, which as far as our religiously-impartial

---

23 By now, you should trust me when I am making a claim.

government should be concerned is for no other reason than because of superstitions.

Ultimately, the right to sell oneself as a prostitute is something that should be considered an inalienable right that no government has the right to take away. After all, aren't we all prostitutes in some way? Work is work. I do not think that humans were meant to work in cubicles or to sit for extended periods, but it is a job that people all over the world do every day. Some of these women--and men--are just trying to make a living, and believe it or not some of them actually enjoy their work. I have no wish to go into the details of how I know this... just take my word for it. I know some people who know people who willingly quit college so that they could sleep with people for money as prostitutes.

However, let us get to the heart of the matter: If there is anything that should be illegal, it is the cruel practice of pimping. Kidnapping, coercion, doping, rape, battery, and withholding payment are illegal for a good reason: they violate the right of another person to live freely. For the love of God... prostitutes are the victims here! If we legalized the sex-trade, then prostitutes across the country would have nobody to hide from. They could unionize, set standards, look out for each other, crack down on abusers and bullies, and put the pimps who give pimping a bad name in jail where they deserve to be. Oh, and as an added bonus, the government gets to collect some taxes for... I don't know, children's hospitals. Everybody wins!

Besides, the sheer hypocrisy of the damned nanny's no-no to prostitution is enough to make me wish I purchased a hat just so I have something to vomit into. If a woman has sex with a man for money she is made into a whore, a criminal, and eventually an enemy of the state. Yet, when a woman has sex with many men for money with a camera rolling… she is made into a porn star.

Something is not right here, and it is pissing me off the more that I think about it.

Jesus Christ…

Enough!

V

Really? Seriously, check right now to see if the government took your guns.

What irritates me so much about the debate over gun ownership is how much time both sides of the issue spend slinging shit at each other like the apes that they are. The handful of shit was a weapon long beform the firearm, but you never hear people talk about that being pried out of their cold, dead hands. Why all the anger? Or better yet, why all the shit-smearing? Probably because "arms" is a term used so loosely that any rational debate over the subject is impossible. It is yet another philosophical argument that nobody can win, and that the state would be wise to stay the fuck out of. As such, I believe the nanny has no right to tell us what toys we can't play with as long as we are responsible gun owners.

Hmmm...

However, therein does lie a question: What is a responsible gun owner?

Well, again, this is impossible to answer and I am not even going to pretend to attempt to. This is the type of bullshit we have been putting up with all our lives, and I consider any attempt to rationalize with the irrational a complete waste of life. It is for the sake of all of us that I insist we retire this argument by acknowledging that, right now, we enjoy the right to keep and bear arms. That's how it's written, so let's leave the matter at that. If anyone says otherwise, simply exercise your First Amendment right to tell whoever you disagree with to go fuck themselves.

I will in the same vein, though, demand that responsible gun ownership be taken just as seriously by those who distribute guns as well as those who purchase them. Naturally, this is something that I don't think our government should enforce because common sense should make federal regulation unnecessary. If you sell an assault rifle to a 5-year-old, odds are you are both going to wind up in the news thanks to your, Jesus... epic stupidity. If you put an atomic weapon up for sale, odds are you acquired it illegally. If someone asks you for armor-piercing bullets, there might be a good chance that they plan to pierce armor with them. This isn't too much to ask, is it? It's called taking pride in your work. Try it sometime, because you're giving gun owners a bad image when you don't.

However, I will say that the biggest dumbasses when it comes to this debate have got to be gun manufacturers. Seriously, how hard is it to put a label on your products that reads: "May kill people." How many of you would like to brag in commercials that your brand of firearms only kills the bad guys. Imagine the countless marketing opportunities you fools are allowing to slip through your fingers! If you above all made the most effort to keep your products out of the wrong hands, there would be no debate over who kills people: people.

In short, the status quo regarding gun ownership is as good as 200 years' worth of debate, bullshit, and more bullshit is going to make it. Leave things the way they are, and accept that it is too late for even the nanny state to take away our guns, ammo belts, and fucking badass bandanas. You gun owners have nothing to fear from the government, so quit fooling yourselves.

All you guys really have to fear are yourselves. So, you know, don't do anything stupid.

VI

"The mother of idiots is always pregnant."
– Italian proverb

All right... For the record, I specifically put this chapter after the one about guns because it baffles my mind how many people identify themselves as pro-life and pro-gun. Nothing personal, I just think that's fucking hysterical.

[Laughter]

Okay. Let's have a serious talk about breastfeeding.

Seven years ago, a 33-year-old immigrant named Jacqueline Mercado and her boyfriend were arrested on child pornography charges punishable up to 20 years in prison. The police searched their home, held them in prison on $22,500 bail, and a state child welfare worker made off with their children. According to Jacqueline, the state "ripped out my heart... Even if we get them back, I don't know how we'll recover from what's been done."

Her boyfriend, a hospital technician in their native land, was understandably pissed off with their new country as well once he learned what was up. The "pornography" amounted to nothing more than a picture of Jacqueline breastfeeding her infant son after bath time.

Seriously.[24]

Ladies and gentlemen, this is how ass-backwards our country is about breastfeeding from the individual prude all the way up to the state level.[25] The fact that something like this can and did happen in our land in this century is beyond appalling. It's...

---

24 Thomas Korosec, "1-Hour Arrest," *Dallas Observer*, April 17, 2003.
25 Albeit Texas.

FUCK YOU!!!

There, I said it.

You know, it would be funny how our culture chooses to treat the breast if it wasn't also so goddamn pathetic. Entire national treasuries have been made off of the swollen mammaries of actresses, weatherwomen, super heroines, and some awful, awful singers this past week alone. There are more bras in our country than suspensions for bridges, and the scientific community has probably spent more time perfecting breast augmentation than the artificial heart. Boobs gloriously grace our billboards, commercials, magazine covers, comic books, beaches, award ceremonies, and the mud flaps of our proudest trucks. And yet the minute one mother starts using them for their natural purpose she immediately becomes subjected to sneering at best and goddamn law enforcement at worst.

How did it come to this? How did our government ever make it their business to pluck an infant from his mother's breast for any reason, never mind this reason? How could even the nanny state lower itself to such a point it would lump private breastfeeding in the same category as child pornography, even if accidently?

Well, according to the history books, the reason is...

No.

I am not even going to attempt to rationalize such irrational behavior. This is sick, obscene stuff we are talking about here, and an insult to our species to treat breasts in such a way.

The public has to get over its fixation with public breastfeeding, fast, because you assholes are to blame for the sorry state of this twisted nanny with live with.

Oh, what a sick, twisted world for our children to inherit.

For shame, you sick bastards. They're just boobs. Deal

with them. I will not stand one more mother having to suffer at the hands of our wretched hostess simply because your have a fucking dilemma over whether or not to get aroused over an exposed breast in public. Hell, do your realize that it was not until 100 years ago that this was even considered taboo? Before that, it was considered a sign of youthfulness and purity for a woman to display breasts. It wasn't until the stuck-up ages that assholes like you came around that upper class women looked down their noses at lower class women with their breasts out, and decided to cover up. They "denied" the world their venom-sapped breasts, and as such created the present perception of breasts, even for breastfeeding, as obscene.

You, my obscene readers, are their legacy.

For shame.

VII

"The reason why so many people are in such a mental recession is because they fail to comprehend all the good shit their government does for them. If you don't like how we do business, then get your own country."
– Dick David Biggins

Rest assured, there will be no misunderstanding when it comes to where our loyalties lie; at least not in this discourse. Even if you love your country, there is nothing wrong with saying that it can be better. Furthermore, nobody deserves to be in this country any more or less than the next person. If you were born here, then it was for a damn good reason: it was so you could own this country. If you don't like how things are going, then take back what is rightfully yours!

The nanny state has done a pretty good job at making itself appear so omnipotent and out of reach that you would think nothing can stop its momentum. So many ills have transpired for so long in our history: our education, our electors, and so many aspects of life as we know it. Is there really much we can do to correct this current that carries us? Do we have the strength to remake our nation in our own image?

Oh Almighty... YES!

Of course we can, and don't you dare let anybody else tell you otherwise! Our nation is just one among many that has gone through its ups and downs throughout history. To overlook its imperfections would be an insult to the character of its finer qualities. Even if we were to fall into a worst-case scenario with the state we would still have our own strength to fall back onto. We are the ones who are the makers of worlds, and we have the power to remake this nation however we see fit. If anyone demoralizes you or feeds you bullshit about how one vote does not count or how no one person ever made a difference, consider this: you lose 100% of the battles you don't fight.

Don't grumble; speak. Don't tolerate; endure. Don't opinionate; do.

The secret to getting things done is to act, so what the fuck are you waiting for! You only live once, and if you wait too long... you'll be dead.

Do not allow your cause of death to be inactivity. History is thick with the graves of the unimportant.

Book II: The Quadrivial
Arithmetic

I

"Oh God, how I love this country..."
– The Barrator, by Ciampolo

Useless, useless words…

It is so easy for those who rape and plunder this country to smile condescendingly upon those they've exploited and shamelessly claim their love and allegiance to their common land. The love they possess is not that of a fraternal band or common will with their many countrymen, but that of an arachnid to a fly, a virus for its host, a lion for a gazelle, or a child toward its wet-nurse. They do not love this country, and they most certainly do not love their fellow countryman. All they like about this place are the countless crimes their government, our government, allows them to get away with every day, and that is the only reason why they choose to call this land their home.

The very ones who steered this country to the brink of financial ruin are the ones our government protects the most. At first these men in suits swore that the government was the cause of all our problems; that the state had grown too large and had become a plague upon us all. In truth, these men did not want to shrink the government: just reform it to their benefit. It was an exercise in venture capital, and our government was just another institution that they had yet to conquer. Together this cabal of businesses, entrepreneurs, and super-rich staged a bloodless coup against our country so successfully that today it is almost impossible for most people to imagine a world without them. They have turned our financial center into a corrupted, blackened heart and infected every vein of our infrastructure, leaving the staggering, emaciated remains of our economy to wander aimlessly into the new century.

They are the ones who did this: the Oligarchs. The plutocrats. They ransomed our economy to our government so they could profit from their own failure. They have borrowed more than our economy could have ever possibly sustained, lined their pockets with the silk of countless subsidies, and they have warped the function of our government into a welfare state for the super-rich. They, these privileged few, have succeeded beyond the wildest dreams of their predecessors. Not only has the government made them larger and more powerful than ever, our entire economy has grown dependent on them.

This is the nanny state in its wickedest, cruelest form: a nanny that will only coddle the super-rich.

A corporate welfare state.

II

"When I sit back and think about all the good that we have done--subprime lending, refinancing, and all the leverage anyone could ask for--I sometimes get the urge to pause and take in the world around me. I swivel in my chair, walk right up to my window, press my hand against the glass, and look down at all the little people milling about their quiet lives. Then I close my eyes, lean my lips into the glass, and remind them in a gentle, loving tone: 'You owe me.'"

– Reginaldo degli Scrovegni

Bankers, brokers, barons, businessmen, entrepreneurs, captains of industry and trade: in the end, they are all just farmers. Farmers of humanity.

While the common planter can only lay claim to the crops he sows, these farmers of humanity live in a system where the children of every corner of our nation, and possibly every nation, is theirs to harvest. Their unbridled wealth is virtually impossible to duplicate unless Fortuna granted you the unfair advantage of being born into their families. The open sewer of their corruption is designed to trickle upward through every infrastructure of our society: business, government, and even faith. The financial ruin of their speculation spreads like a cancer through our currency, devaluing every dollar of every person helplessly anchored to it. They own this country, and their insatiable greed knows no bounds. These are the captains of our economy: thieves, rogues, and criminals. However, they will never pay the price for any of their misdeeds. No, because our laws are designed to empower the rich--commensurate to the amount of wealth they have!

There is an invisible line in our society that I call 'the Line of Liberty' that allows you to get away with virtually any crime as long as you possess enough wealth. You can stab your wife to death and murder a total stranger as long as you are deemed too popular for the state to execute. You can openly and unabashedly profit off wars that you started as long as you are good enough to be the best in the business. You can rob a person of everything as long as you do it 50,000 times and all at once. You can steal the single most powerful throne in our government, the presidency, as long as you surround yourself with enough men and women willing to sell their souls to their party and publicly prostitute every dignity of their offices just to see the other guy lose. Hell, even as I write this, a billionaire has been accused of repeatedly raping his underage step-daughter for years. Do you think our system will ever allow him to go to jail? Less wealthy men have gotten away with worse in this land, and you know it.

However, no matter what you do, you must not question their patriotism. No matter how many of their countrymen get screwed over, do not doubt that they love their country. No matter how many of their own soldiers are needlessly killed, do not accuse them of not supporting our troops. No matter how many deals they make with enemies of this country, do not call them traitors as long as they are the ones in charge. And above all else--no matter how many families they drive into ruin, no matter how many children may grow sick and die, no matter how many veterans die alone and homeless, no matter how many of your friends become enslaved by debt, no matter how many houses they foreclose, no matter how many strikes they break, no matter how many businesses they ruin, no matter how many leaders they assassinate--please, do not accuse them of not valuing life. Of course they do. They love life.

Humanity has become their cattle.

III

"Breaking the law is not illegal as long as you find a way
to do it legally."
– Sir Catello di Rosso Gianfigliazzi

At this point I might as well share what I was able to find out
about the current financial crisis after doing some private
investigating. While I will admit that my study began as
nothing more than an attempt to score some business-
class cocaine, what I obtained to go with it promises to be
nothing short of a golden fleece of intellectual fuzziness, if
that makes sense.

Please don't judge me because I do this for your sake. I
have obtained this cocaine for the sole purpose of putting
myself in the same exact mindset as the businessmen who
corrupted this country in the first place. It is in front of
me right now, in four thin lines. In my left hand is a black
credit card, and in my right a rolled up one hundred-dollar
bill that I have been assured was obtained through TARP
funds.

For the sake of mankind, I do this for you. To better
understand man's vices, and man's worth… Here we go.

Done.

Nothing yet. My nose does feel kind of fuzzy.

Not-

Okay, it's kicking in.

And…

THERE.

I feel it…

I…

…

Holy shit…

[Four hours later]

My interview is completed, and I have my information. While it may ramble a bit, please believe me when I say that I have just spent the last several hours observing its every single atom with diamond-like precision. I have seen the beast, all of it, and now hours are passing like years. My heart is beating so fast that I cannot control my left hand. I cannot sit without my eyes darting every which way. For the sake of my purpose, I must resort to dictations:

Shortly after the terrorist attacks ten years ago the government took steps to prevent our nation from ever having to shut down the stock market again. This was meant as a safeguard; an insurance policy made without the consent of the people and without the public knowledge of how vulnerable our economy was in the wake of disaster. It was agreed that the stock exchange would be empowered by our government to operate remotely; from the workplace, from home, from anywhere in the world. Instead of having to wave your hands on the floor like a madman, the state empowered a select few of our nation's businesses to rebuild our entire economy as they saw fit. These men were made gods.

This opened up a whole new frontier of online speculation; an opportunity for those of insatiable greed to break every law in the book all over again, only this time with the government's approval. This, my dear reader, was the beginning of the end of our economy.

Out of fear, the state made these thieves into our vanguard, and it should come to the surprise of no sound mind that they immediately used this power to pull off one of the greatest heists in history: the theft of our country. This is the reason why the rich became richer, the poor became poorer, and the middle class was forced into nothing short of a siege. The keys of the kingdom were handed over to the same criminals our government had been too afraid to imprison. Out of the ruins of our fallen towers they built a second Tower of Babel to rule the world from, only this time fully aware that there would be no God to stop them. They were now too big to fail, too large and too corrupt an infestation to amputate. They used this opportunity to deliberately drive us deeper into the ground, make themselves stronger than ever, and have our highest courts declare that they be treated as individuals: supermen among men. Thanks to the intervention of our government, these fallen angels were given wings.

While this is not the nanny state at its cruelest, it is certainly the nanny state at its stupidest. In its attempt to keep us safe, they hired wolves to watch us while we slept.

IV

"I believe in whatever I want to believe. That way, even if I am wrong I can still believe that I am right and that the rest of the world is wrong."
– Ciappo Ubriachi

There are some schools of economic thought that believe being objective is an ism; that it is possible for the human mind to rise above its own consciousness and reshape the world as an irrepressible, existential actor. They believe that anybody can scrape the sky or shake the planet without concern for anyone other than themselves. They believe that it is possible for men--and women--to rule over us like Atlas or Prometheus.

It is fitting that they choose to associate themselves so closely with figures from mythology.

Objectivism is nothing short of a religion, and one of the most self-righteously annoying ones at that. Think tanks are their churches and their economic summits their podiums. Their books have become their bibles and their fictionalized ideals their gods. They have enjoyed a near-monopoly of our economy for the past half-century, fostering an entire generation of economic minds who have steered our country toward its present stage without giving even the slightest doubt, concern, or fuck for what the rest of the world thought about them. How were they able to do this? How were they able to so change this country? Easily. They believed that the only moral economic philosophy in this world was to let the wealthiest people do whatever they wanted, and the super-rich propagated this philosophy with a crusader's zeal.

The reason why this economic policy is flawed is because not all men are created equal. It gives the human character more credit than it deserves because it works only with fictionalized ideals. The human is not a controllable test subject, and therefore cannot be tested within an environment that assumes human flaws are invariable and consistent, or even nonexistent. We are greedy and prodigal sons, ignorant and intelligent creatures, creative and destructive forces, and, above all else, flawed creations and infinitely unique in consistently inconsistent ways. Objectivists believe that it is possible for humanity to obtain perfection, and that it all starts with them; that they cannot be wrong, they must not be wrong, because they are so sure that they are right.

They live in more denial than most of the rational people of this world. They believe that the wealthiest of men can be trusted and that the poorest are untrustworthy. They believe that anybody can obtain whatever they want without somebody standing in their way. They believe that a good idea will always triumph over the bad as long as you stick to it with all you've got. Well, I am sorry to report to all these 'moralists' that even rich people can be dumb as a stone, that some people will forever be denied a fair opportunity due to race, faith, gender, and/or sexual orientation, and that even dumb ideas can stick around for quite a while. If you want a good example of this, look no further than objectivism.

These are the people who helped destroy our country. They empowered some of the most untrustworthy, corruptible corporate criminals in our country with unlimited power and unregulated oversight simply because they believed that greed is not a trait to be associated with the super-rich. What… the fuck… were they thinking?

Make no mistake, some of these philosophers are very intelligent men and women, but they became so infatuated with their own egos that all they have become the living Narcissus. They have faltered in their quest for glory like the Giants who stormed Olympus. They have forced countless innocents into hostile waters in a mad flight comparable only to that of Ulysses. They have ruined our entire economy without remorse, regret, or even the slightest hint of financial responsibility... and it was all so that they could preserve an idea that, who would have guessed, kinda made them all rich.

Let these mutual intellectual masturbators circle-jerk to their hearts' content. They are allowed to indulge in their mythological fantasies all they want. All I ask is that you, the rational, not fall for their trap. These prophets brought upon us a doomsday that they predicted would be a Paradise. They infiltrated the highest levels of our banks and treasuries to steer us toward a collision course they helped create. They are unfair, unkind bullies whose mental health suggests a narcissistic apathy toward humanity on the same level as serial killers, megalomaniacs, and certain rodents.

These assholes are allowed to live their lives in as much delusion as they please. However, that does not give them the right to force our country back into their failed experiment. Everybody is entitled to their own opinions, but nobody is entitled to their own facts. These economists had their shot at rebuilding this nation into their Paradise, and when they did, it crashed down upon us all thanks to the darker natures within all our souls: ignorance, impotence, and hatred.

If they still think that they're onto something after so spectacular a failure, then let's just keep things simple and agree that they're a cult.

V

"We are entitled to everything we earn, including our entitlements."
  – Vitaliano di Iacopo Vitaliani

At long last, we come to the vile, putrid heart of the corporate conspiracy against this great nation of ours: the establishment of a permanent, unquestioned, and virtually omnipotent corporate welfare state.

It is almost impossible to picture a world where corporate welfare would actually make sense. After all, why should some of the most successful businesses in our country be entitled to anything from the government? After all, a true laissez-faire market should not favor government intervention of any kind. Tell me, why in the world should the already-bloated nanny state expand her role to foster corporations and businesses as if they were princes and kings; gods, even?

Oh, yeah... because they made the state their nanny.

The idea behind corporate welfare is that the state should be empowered to reward businesses with grants as if they brought home a good report card. These monies, which basically total the maximum amount their lobbyists were able to squeeze out of our treasury, is supposed to be used by said company to expand their business and hire more employees. It's like pouring gasoline onto a fire in the hopes that all the smoke will make it rain. This, my dear reader, is seriously how stupid trickle-down economics is.

Why does it sound ridiculous? Because it is ridiculous. This entire maneuver was nothing short of a blatant, public conquest of our government through decades of financial contributions to candidates that corporations knew they could control like marionettes. They were able to conquer entire states through this method, and eventually all three branches of the government itself. Six years ago they received $57 billion in subsidies. One year later, $92 billion in subsidies.[26] One year after that, the economy started to collapse. One year after that, the economy did collapse, and was supposedly about one $1 trillion in subsidies away from collapsing even more.

My dear readers, who the hell are they fooling? Such reckless, wasteful spending is not the type of thing we should tolerate simply because we see it on the news every single damn day. It is a crime, and you know it, and nothing is being done about it. It is the theft of our riches while our house is burning down. It is a disaster, and injustice, and an affront to us all, and how are these corporations getting away with it? Because we let them.

We let them get away with this because we stood by and did nothing as they tackled and beat the nanny state and essentially made her their slave. They are the true villains in this sorry tale. They are the wealthiest, most powerful, and most dangerous people to all our liberties. They have turned this country into something worse than a plutocracy: they have turned it into their own personal ATM with the common man existing to pay the overdraft fees. All the worse, they are showing absolutely no signs of stopping their endless withdrawal. Whenever they're out of money, they just make the state print more.

However, these arch-villains were not content with turning the wealthiest and most powerful country in the world into their own ATM. No, they also had to turn it into a weapon they could wield to beat down anybody who would dare to stop them. Who are their mortal enemies? Everyone who is not them.

26 Stephen Slivinski, *The Corporate Welfare State: How the Federal Government Subsidizes U.S. Business*, The Cato Institute, 2007.

VI

"I look at my employees and see nothing but hate. I see every one of them unhappy and eager to rise up against me. I see them biding their time, waiting for the right moment to strike. When they do, I will be ready. They may hate me, but I hate them even more."
– Giovanni di Buiamonte

My heart goes out to the unions right now.

It is no secret that the biggest threat to big business has always been organized labor. In the old days the business state dealt with them the easiest way possible: they killed them. They dispatched bullies, strike-breakers, policemen, national guardsmen, and even federal troops whenever they acted up. This was the perfect solution for tackling unions: it deprived them of their leaders, lessened their numbers, and ultimately terrorized their entire work force with the realization of how hopeless it was to rise against them. It was a glorious time in the history of the free market economy, albeit a somewhat hypocritical time since big business was able to do this by having the whole goddamn government in their pocket.

Today's business leaders employ a much more sophisticated method for dealing with unions: elections, laws, and even their control of our high courts. I have no doubt in the world that this is the last route they would have liked to take, but it has nevertheless been able to net them fantastic successes. In just the last few years business leaders were able to convince the highest courts in the land that corporations are individuals,[27] and are thus able to

---

27 *Citizens United v. Federal Election Commission*, 130 U.S. 876 (2010)

enjoy all the liberties of life in this land--except of being drafted, arrested, or executed of course. This has allowed corporations to contribute hundreds of millions, if not billions, of dollars to congressional candidates most likely to... you guessed it, keep the government off their backs. However, it is worth noting that while this may sound like an exercise of free-market economics, corporations are still very much in favor of receiving huge subsidies in tax-payer money. Interestingly, this means that some corporations could have--and likely did--help elect officials loyal to them using the very same corporate welfare the government gave them in the first place. In short, corporations have empowered the government to make them rich, just so they can use their wealth to reshape the government even more to their liking.

You need look no further than the heartland of our country to see what the intention of the corporate welfare state was: the utter destruction of organized labor. It was not even spring thaw before the new governors and elected officials signed into law measures that would cripple the power of organized labor in state after state. Why are they doing this? Why empower the government so as to make the collective power of organized labor illegal? The only plausible explanation is that it was for the best of the state, meaning that, just like the nanny state, it was the government's way of looking out for us.

Naturally, this is utter bullshit.

It is difficult to look at this sordid state of affairs and deduce who is at fault here: the corporate welfare state, or the nanny state. In all honesty, the two have become so intertwined that they are locked in their union of continual intercourse. The two have mated to create an even worse offspring the likes of which we are all victims to. The state has become larger, more powerful than ever, and it has chosen to use its power to declare war on the middle class.

Unless you are too rich to even have time to read books like this, heed my warning when I say this: they hate you. They despise you and insult you and wish you nothing but misery. They want you to be poor, stupid, sick, overweight, and in debt. They want you to be distracted by commercials and freak shows so that your mind is too overwhelmed to know anything other than over-consumption. They want you to own more than you can possibly afford, and they will do all that they can to keep you poor so that you never truly own what is yours. They want your home, your possessions, your family, your future, and everything short of your life simply because they want you to live just enough so that you can work.

Oh my, how they hate you, and how they hate humanity. They have conquered this country, and they will do everything in their power to use it to destroy you.

Their words, not mine.[28]

---

28 Their actions speak footnotes.

VII

"People need to stop bitching about the economy already. Seriously, shut up, already. You sound retarded."
– Former Senator Billiam "Texas" Cheesestake

I believe in a free market, and I believe in it passionately. I believe in laissez-faire economics with all my heart. I believe that humanity will always be cruel, and that there is nothing we can do about it. I believe that the economy is just another realm of the jungle where mad men will ferociously fight for survival. I believe that every man has every right to be as merciful or as cruel with his capital as he wishes. All I ask is that our governments play absolutely no role in choosing sides.

The nanny state has chosen to foster the rich in every single realm of our economy. It has empowered them, showered them with countless riches, and provided them with the best system of welfare that our world has ever seen: a welfare state that will never let them grow ill and frail. These are ordinary men, like you and me, who are being treated as our superiors simply because our state believes that it will be for the good of us all. They have unleashed riot police, strike-breakers, and even federal troops upon us for no other reason than because we dared question their wisdom. They have fined us, arrested us, and even killed us in cold blood for daring to take back what is ours: the work of our hands.

Well, as strange and as sick as this surrogate of the nanny state is, they are bound to us by this one simple fact: they cannot kill us all. They can drive some of us to ruin, but not all of us. They can ruin all of our lives only some of the time and only some of our lives all the time, but never all of our lives all of the time. At the end, they know that they need us more than we will ever need them. They know that for all the men and women they control in our government they will always be outnumbered. They know that as their possessions grow larger they become even more difficult to control. They know that they fear us for the same reason the plantation owners of old feared their slaves: at the end of the day, we outnumber them.

I am not encouraging violence, but I can tell you that revolutions have occurred via people exercising nothing more than their right to not participate. This is a wild, cruel engine of industry we live in, but as long as it continues to run over our innocent, people like me will be there to stand in its way.

And to think that people like me are willing to sacrifice our lives for no other reason than to stand between men and their perverse love for money. Heroes have given their lives in more noble causes than this.

We should all be ashamed of our state for the embarrassment it has become.

Astronomy

I

"Ahhhhhhhhhhhhhhhhhhhhhhhhhhhh!!!!!!!!!!!!"
– Icarus

Challenge: it seems like a good thing to take. After all, how else are we to know our limits unless we test them? I welcome a good challenge, and I challenge anyone to challenge my theories. However, even a good challenge can be an utter waste of everyone's time.

We all hail from a country that has championed space, but for what purpose? Was it for peace? Mankind? Hardly. This new frontier was conquered by our military. Was it for knowledge? Not exactly. We remain more ignorant about our own oceans than the heavens. What was it for, then? What greater purpose motivated our nation to soar to unprecedented heights and plant our flag on one of the greatest trophies anyone could ask for?
Oh yeah... it all started off a dare.

II

"I would rather die than live to see my country lose a good fight."

– King Saul

Have you ever stopped to consider whether or not the Cold War was a war even worth fighting? Our government spent nearly $20 trillion dollars on everything from mind-control experiments to doomsday machines. The lives of more than 100,000 of our soldiers were needlessly sacrificed in mismanaged land wars in Asia we would have been smart to avoid. Millions of civilians around the world were killed by our weapons. Freely-elected government leaders were either deposed or assassinated by our agents. Our nation emerged more in debt than it had ever been in its history, and even 20 years later we have yet to recover from this injury... yet we won! Didn't we?

I challenge anyone who can look at such staggering numbers to make the case that we somehow emerged from this conflict on top. We are dying right now because of the scars of the Cold War. Our citizens are sick and dying because of the partisan squabbling of the Cold War. Hundreds of thousands of veterans are homeless and millions more lives ruined because of the Cold War. Oh, and let's not forget that we inched our planet closer than ever to Armageddon, the destruction of billions of human--and countless plant and animal--lives on our planet, and in some cases over nothing more than human and even animal error.[29]

29 For real. We nearly nuked the whole planet over a goddamn bear. Read more in Rory Colthurst, "Five Wacky Misunderstandings That Almost Caused a Nuclear Holocaust," in *You Might Be a Zombie and Other Bad News: Shocking but Utterly True*

Could any of these scenarios in any way be justified because we also happened to shoot a few monkeys into space in the meantime? Is it worth saying that life in our space has been made better because our government deemed it necessary to utterly destroy life on this planet? Can we honestly have faith in our nanny's decision making after she has shown such utter, dangerous contempt for human life in the past?

I say no. I say that the Cold War and every single one of its expenditures was nothing more than a fool's errand that we were incredibly dumb to be a part of. It was almost like our country had become as naive as Midas when he wished to turn everything he touched into gold. Our government recklessly and dangerously squandered our treasury to its current state, and all for a purpose that I will question the integrity of without question or hesitation.

The Cold War was a fight that we were dumb as dumb fucks for fighting, and it has made the nanny state larger, crueler, and crazier than she has ever been in the process. The nanny state has spent the last several decades looking up into space as a new frontier to expand her domination upon us on the ground.

She. Is. Insane.

Facts, ed. Cracked.com (New York: Plume, 2011) 86.

III

"I still don't know why they named the whole damn thing after me."

– Apollo

I see the Moon as an object of beauty: something for the whole world to share rather than fight over. It is life-changing, a fountainhead of music, poetry, and enlightenment, a miracle of mathematics and nature, and, in a gentle way, loving. It is our planet's life partner, and I love her dearly.

As such, why the hell have we subjected her to such cruel experimentation? Sending men to the Moon did not bring us world peace. On the contrary, it is difficult to picture a more terrible time in our history than when we walked on the Moon: countless peacemakers had been assassinated, we had a would-be dictator for president, and our nation was bogged in perhaps the most unforgivably wasteful, immoral war in our history. There was nothing but hatred and distrust for our government, and its iron grip had become so merciless that by the new year we had come to the point that even unarmed college students were deemed enemies of the state. Yes, it was the perfect time in our history to waste fortunes and ignore the more important cries of our people just to make our enemies look bad.

The Egyptians built monuments to their kings visible from space. Not to be outdone in a stupid contest, we placed a monument to our kings in space. It took us more than 4,000 years to one-up them, and for what? The single greatest achievement of the nanny state: a monument that we cannot see or visit, and might as well not even exist.

The Apollo program cost a total of roughly $110 billion today.[30] I know that by now you have been desensitized by such numbers, but just this one time I ask you to focus on them. Look at this figure and picture what our nation could have done with it; the more pressing issues of the era that could have been addressed. Picture the cries that so many people from the time, many of them asking for nothing more than that they be treated equally, fairly. Or that they not be sent off to fight a war against an enemy they didn't know and had no reason to kill. (Just to reinforce, all of this could have been done for free.) Or better yet, this is money that we could have not even taxed in the first place! It could have gone back to you, the citizen: the person who it belonged to in the first place. Instead, the government chose to tax it from your pocket so that it could be shot into space.

Also, I know that some of you are seduced by the achievement of this era. Walking on the Moon... Tell me, did you ever do it? Do you think you will ever get to do it in your lifetime? Has it really made life easier for every single person on this country? Hell, even some of the men who walked on the Moon came back to Earth depressed.[31] Well, I'm not depressed; I'm angry. I'm mad! I'm furious! What the hell were they doing on the Moon on our dime in the first place! $110 billion? Why not $110 trillion dollars? Why not everything we owned and everything that

---

30 Congressional Budget Office, *A Budgetary Analysis of NASA's New Vision for Space Exploration* (September 2004).
31 Andrew Smith, *Moondust: In Search of the Men Who Fell to Earth* (New York: HarperCollins, 2005).

we could own? Was it really worth the cost? Was it really worth any cost? Oh, and the best part about this decision: we, the citizens, had no choice in it.

I sometimes wonder if instead we lived on Mars. Perhaps the idea of landing on two moons would have made the whole endeavor seem like half the achievement. Would we have expanded our schoolyard bullying into space and fought over each other's floating rocks? Would the Cold War have reverted to our moon vs. their moon? (And naturally, each side thinking their moon was better?) What if we had three moons, or five moons, or eight, or thirteen? Or maybe even 21 moons, like Uranus? Would it have seemed even stupider for us to land on any one of those moons at a time when there were clearly better things we could have been doing on this planet, such as reigning in our insane government before it brought us any closer to debt and destruction?

Oh, how I envy Uranus. It has 21 moons and no problems. We have one and it has driven men mad.

IV

Astronomy is a science. There is no denying that. However,
it is important to not let astronomy interfere with astrology,
which we all know is bullshit.

I am well aware of the maniacal cults who stare at the
stars and pretend to read them for doomsday predictions.
These people are simple, strange, and ultimately soon parted
of their time and money by an entire host of merchants
eager to exploit their stupidity. All the same, I think it just
as foolish to examine something as costly and unsafe as
space travel as means to any kind of wealth or fortune.
No matter how much iron or gold is floating around this
planet, I think it is pretty safe to say that it will never be
worthy to search for it here. Even if we do find water on
distant planets, we will probably never be able to drink it.
And--the big one--if we find life, I am confident that it
will be no more intelligent than us. However, I will praise
them for not being stupid enough to leave their planet in
the first place.

The fact that our government continues to this day
countless programs for space exploration seriously make
me wonder if astronomy has taken the place of astrology.
We have yet to discover the many secrets of this planet, but
we have already jumped off it to see whatever else is out
there. I view this as silly as stopping a book at its midpoint

just to read as many books as you can find to see if there
is anything else just as good. Yes, I am aware that it is for
the purpose of scientific discovery, but I cannot shake the
idea that it is based too heavily on luck and fortune. Space
exploration is a crap shoot, and I do not like the idea of our
government gambling our money on it one bit.

Our own world is too wild and diverse to explore in a
thousand lifetimes, never mind one visit. We still have much
to learn here, and so many of our greatest discoveries were
done without the government's expense. I am not saying
this to be cynical, but to address just how far the state has
overextended itself, and, as a result, weakened us all. How
in the world is a probe shot into the deepest regions of
space in any way a matter of national importance? How
is it vital to our government and every one of us here to
test the effects of a human being in zero-gravity? What
good does an international space station do for us warring
nations on Earth? We are still here and we still have the
same problems as before, only this time we're just a little
bit more broke due to all the damn space exploration our
government has been doing.

The state believes that its job is to better serve mankind.
The nanny state, on the other hand, believes that it is the
government's job to be our dictator. As long as they continue
to spend billions of our tax dollars searching for fortune
from planet to planet, I say that they are no different than
the kings and queens who wasted their people's money
consulting astrologers.

V

"No! You must not take the stars from us! If we do not read them, who will! Oh, how did I not see this coming? Take your hands off me! Stop this! You need us! You need me! [Screaming]"

– Manto

Monopolies are not very easy to manage. I know this because I have managed some in my past--albeit on a much smaller scale. As such, I am a firm believer that the cosmos are slightly more difficult to govern than our planet, which is why I think our government has been wasting its time in their near-monopoly of space travel.

Perhaps the most prevalent argument against cutting funding for space exploration is that the field will collapse without federal support. I challenge this notion. Has not aviation benefited immensely from being turned over to the public sector? Has not the competiveness of rival businesses actually spurred aviators and pioneers to soar to new heights? Yes, the government has played a role in getting work started, but as much as I lament the large part it has played I see no problem in the government allowing the entire field of space exploration to be turned over to the people.

Think about it: how many innovations have been made in the last decade alone out of the endless wars corporations fight with each other? Imagine if the entire Space Race had been privatized. Instead of nations, it could be businesses in a mad flight to use their enormous wealth to plant their flag on the Moon, Mars, and beyond. I do not say this with cynicism or even regret, because it returns this power to the people. Technology has matured to the point where the nanny state can finally surrender its iron grip on the industry and let the free market take over.

Yes, I am aware that this will probably lead to all sorts of corruption, exploitation, and the inevitable advertising. Yes, space exploration may all just become a sick joke in the end, but at least it is one less responsibility that the nanny state has forced upon us, the taxpayers. We no longer need our government to keep this child ensnared. All they need to do is sever its umbilical cord, and I have the fullest confidence that space exploration will go down as just another chapter in the growing and changing history of aviation.

Instead, the state has chosen to preserve it like a doting parent, smothering it with unwarranted attention. We have already extended our fingertips to our system's greatest horizons, and yet our government is still so myopic as to look upon us as a nation. If anything, the Space Race has succeeded at making our state less significant. It has shown how unimportant and futile our own borders are. We are one planet, not one nation. We are one species, not one people. We have the right to exercise our science and technology however we please, and the government is in no position to tell us what toys we are still too young to play with.

Please, my dear reader, take back what is yours. Our money is lost, but at least it was spent on something that we can use to regain our losses. Don't petition the government to hand over all its science and technology to the private sector: demand it. It is ours, and we should be the ones to write our own future.

Do not let the ego and ambitions of one nation keep us stuck on this rock like an anchor. The world is not our oyster; the universe is.

VI

"Everybody's an alien!"
– [unidentified homeless man on the street]

Oh, before we leave the subject of Astronomy behind us, I might as well take the time to address some of the new problems the state may have burdened us with. Namely, the potentially suicidal course our government has charted in search for intelligent life.

Our culture likes to project itself as the best thing in the universe. 'Oh, look at that fancy car... look at this hot body... look at these awesome savings...' best in the universe. Yes, it's all a lie. I mean, the Sun alone kind of puts everything to be found on this planet to shame, but there is always the ever-present danger that there exists an intelligent life form out there better than us at every single field of human technology, including destroying all humans.

As I write, there are scopes scoping and probes probing the deepest bowels of our galaxy in search of someone or something that is kinda like us--and all at the tax-payers' expense. Why, in the world, are they doing this? Don't they know that exploration is the first step in conquest! How do we know that looking back at us is not someone as crazy and insatiable as ourselves: alpha-men bent on destruction and searching for new life! They could be using our probes and our radio signals as animal tracks to hunt us down, destroy us, and ultimately hang us up as their trophies!

All the worse, we have spent the last several decades broadcasting into space, everything they would ever need to know about our military defenses. They have countless examples of how we defended ourselves against aliens, monsters, tripods, robots, and some less-original ideas. They have seen how we function, and they can study our methods. In short, the more we think and talk about aliens, they more vulnerable we make ourselves to them. In fact, it is with a heavy heart that I even write this into this book right now, but I am willing to risk the world's destruction by aliens rather than live one more weekend in this accursed nanny state.

The nanny state thinks that this is all for our welfare. They think that searching and signaling for intelligent life will be awesome. They think if we make contact with extraterrestrial life it might actually make those hundreds of billions of dollars blown worth it. It does not. Every single penny they spend in their search makes us weaker and hurls us further and further towards disaster. We need to stop talking about this now and forever, starting now!

We must!

...

...But, it is already too late. No matter what we do, the probes we have dispatched are already out there, sending messages and broadcasts and showing pictures of what we look like when we're naked. They have all they need to know to examine our bodies, find out where we're from, and ultimately use all the helpful postcards we sent them to enslave and/or annihilate every single one of us. This is not paranoia, although I admit it may sound like it is. Just know that every single thing I have shared with you is the truth.

However, there is one glimmer of hope for us that I see in this mess. By dooming us all to the inevitable alien onslaught, the state has made it impossible for them to threaten us with anything ever again. Things cannot be any worse, and that puts the ball squarely into our court. Without hope, we can finally take the nanny state on in full knowledge that things are not going to get any better if we do nothing.

Advantage: us.

VII

"...It's bad."
– Tiresias

Give the state enough power, and they'll wipe out humanity with it: this is the lesson of the past half-century.

Space exploration has made our lives poorer and none the wiser. All we have learned is how ignorant we have always been. All we have discovered is our own insignificance. All we have contributed to the cosmos is garbage.

This, my dear reader, is the legacy of our state's space program. We could have simply not cared when our rivals first jumped into space, but instead we took it the way any schoolchild would: as a dare. We dared ourselves to be even more wasteful and stupid than our rivals, and it worked. We showed the whole planet just how far out we were willing to take a bad idea. We have spent nearly $1 trillion dollars doing this, lost more than one dozen of our countrymen, and killed an untold number of monkeys in the process.

If we do come in contact with extraterrestrials, let us hope that they are more merciful toward us than the nanny state ever was to this universe.

However, I will admit that this does make me pause. After all, the nanny state is the product of humans. Is this truly the fate we deserve? I look out my window as I ponder this now, but instead see nothing but an overcast sky staring back at me: no answer from above. I am forced to look at Earth, at the trees and the houses and the people around me, and, right then and there, my faith is restored in humanity. I know what the answer is: We do not deserve this.

The Space Race was never put to a vote! Our people

never had a fair platform to protest! This whole goddamn adventure was done against our will! Oh, I cannot lose faith in humanity because humanity has been made victim by a cabal of cruel people who would gladly destroy this whole planet if just to preserve the stupid little life they have been given. It is unfair that this is what the Fates had in store for us, but history has no shortage of demagogy or tyrants. We are all human, we are all flawed, and we are all mortal. We are allowed to make mistakes, but we should try to learn from them.

The crimes of the state in this instance are unforgivable. They have wasted our treasury and opened the door for an alien invasion to wipe out all life as we know it on Earth. However, the dark storm has not come yet. It is cloudy outside, but it is not raining.

Maybe if we were able to do something about this contemptible nanny state between now and the impending invasion, the aliens might find a new breed of humanity much stronger and smarter than anything they would have imagined. Perhaps we could win that fight as well.

Perhaps...

...

Yeah, perhaps.

Music

I

"I love art. It makes for good smashing."
– Attila the Hun

Under no circumstances will I ever tell a person that their child is too ugly to be seen in public. Behind their backs, yes, I will say that and have, but never in public. That's just rude, and frankly it makes you come off as a dick.

My feelings towards art are no different at all. Being a bit of an artist myself, I feel nothing but love for all of mankind's artistic creations. I love the good and the bad. Hell, I even love the untalented. For me, art is not nearly as beautiful as the fact that somebody created it; that both the art and the artist exist. Art stands as all the proof you need that, yes, somebody had an idea and went with it. Somebody created. Somebody acted, and their art is the product of it. This is the reason why I cherish every piece of art from the sculpture to the specks of stone on the floor; from the portrait to the empty paint can; from the symphony to the out-of-tune hum. These are all children of the human mind, and no matter how stupid they are or how annoying they sound, they deserve just as much a place on this planet as that ugly child from earlier.

However, once again the thoughtless, careless, worthless nanny state has to demonstrate its brainlessness on the subject of art. The state, whose sole function is to deprive every one of us of the liberties that make us human, actually has the gall to apply the same cruelty towards the work of the Muses. Our art is not the work of this world, but the product of human enlightenment! It is the second miracle of humanity! It is the grandchild of life! How dare the state stick its shit-stained snout into our fountains! These are our works, our creations, our children, and I refuse to let anybody, man or machine, take away their right to exist!

I do not know what maxim is used or what standard they are held to: this is all just a bullshit philosophy to me. I have no patience nor will to reason with the unreasonable. I am insulted, offended, and infuriated by the very thought of this debate. My hands are curled as if begging for something to strangle. My fingernails are itching to scratch enemies. My brow is bent and my teeth snapping around me. Every muscle in my body is quivering with rage. My heart is pumping with anger like an overfed furnace. I am using every shred of reason left in me to spell the words I need to record this, but believe me when I say that I cannot hold out much longer. I am mad. Furious. Livid. Fuming.

Okay, I need to break something...

[Later]

Holy shit... I think I just created a modern art masterpiece.

Okay, I feel better now.

Let's get back to why that ugly child is not so ugly after all.

II

"Art is meant to be judged. I prefer my judgment to be final."
— Dionysius the Elder

I think it is most important that we understand just how intimately the nanny state has chosen to force itself upon the independence of our artists. Let the following facts be submitted as proof of this:

The state has infringed upon our inalienable right to express ourselves freely.

The state has refused to hear cases and appeals to judgment which they have viewed unnecessary or unimportant.

The state has refused to pass amendments guaranteeing the right to free speech through art in specific instances and cases.

The state has called together public bodies for the sole purpose of debating what is and is not art.

The state has threatened to cut off funding to some of our greatest cities' greatest museums for no other reason than because they disagreed with their catalogues.

The state has refused for a long time to properly debate this subject.

The state has restricted the sale and distribution of art that they deem to be pornographic.

The state has censored their own state-sponsored artwork.

The state has forced our judges to uphold anachronistic cultural dogmas as law.

The state has erected bodies and committees for the sole purpose of exploiting this debate for partisan advantage.

The state has kept, at times of peace, a ready and waiting military force ready to arrest those who dissent their laws.

The state has forced their will upon our artists.

The state has placed a double standard upon our artwork based on sexual and cultural discrimination.

The state has stolen private artwork and impounded it as evidence.

The state has censored privately-published writing, and restricted its sale and distribution.

The state has censored privately-produced music, and restricted its sale and distribution.

The state has censored privately-produced entertainment, and restricted its sale and distribution.

The state has censored privately-produced toys and trinkets, and restricted their sale, distribution, and enjoyment.

The state has imposed its laws upon our private business and bedrooms.

The state has imposed its laws upon our thoughts and imaginings.

The state has imposed its laws upon our own biological urges.

The state has imposed its laws upon our words and speech.

Also, let it be written here and now that a culture's collective creative spirit has always been the single greatest threat to an authorial administration. Everyone from the Pharaohs to the Caesars to the Papacy has used their powers as an excuse to impose a new order upon their culture in a matter they best see fit. This has always been done at the expense of the artistic mind, subverting it, silencing it, and forcing it to change its ways or face the consequences. This has led to the silence of great speakers, the imprisonment of authors, the arrest of artists, the censorship of musicians, and the loss of countless works of art. All the worse, this has perverted the human experience and forced culture down a path where our natural, artistic creations have been sabotaged, shunned, and destroyed. They have brainwashed our masses, conditioning us to accept and reject what they see fit for the state rather than let us act openly and freely in accordance to the powers that inspire us to create.

This, my dear reader, is the martial law the state has forever imposed upon the artistic community.

III

"This vile and degenerate artwork has no place in a decent society!"
— Mayor Julius Little

Does a single person here claim to have a conscience clean enough to preside as judge over what is or is not artwork? I have no delusions over what is or is not artwork; I simply create. How the rest of the world judges it is not important. My creations are what they are.

However, I will again and again object to those who claim that their position within the state somehow empowers them to make larger, more sweeping charges over what is or is not art over the culture they were there to serve. Firstly, every single elected official has been just as drunk, stupid, sexually experimental, and even at times as law-breaking as your average citizen. Nobody is above the law, not even them, and thus I find it hypocritical for any one of them to act as a vanguard for a culture that they too share in its decadence.

Take, for example, a recent case where one of our nation's most famous museums was nearly closed because one exhibit offended the mayor. I do not need to go into what the exhibit was because no words of mine can describe it. Nor can the words of any language. Or any person. It simply existed. It was art. It was a creation that deserved to have a platform just as well as any other, and one respected institution deemed it significant enough to warrant their greatest platform. The mayor of this town chose to use everything within his power to put the museum "out of business" simply because he did not agree with this exhibit.

He preached about religion as if he actually went to church every day. He talked about family values and decency even though he was hard at work maintaining a hardcore sexual rendezvous on the side. He talked about law and virtue even though his law enforcers policed the city like a corrupt military. He lectured us about our children as if his kids still spoke to him. He spoke about art as if he even knew the meaning of the word.

Museums, the home of Muses, just might be the closest we ever come to building a Paradise on this world. They are the closest things that I feel comfortable to calling places of worship. They are our greatest creations. They are our truest treasures. They are our most vulnerable children, and I will do anything to keep them safe.

By very wary, my dear reader, of anyone who uses their power to destroy museums. Those who do are tyrants of this world, and the single, greatest threat to the independent mind.

IV

"Destroy their books. Bury their scholars. Erase them from existence."

– Qin Shi Huang

On the subject of literary censorship, I am afraid I must be brief. Even as I write I must look this way and that for my own safety.

It is no secret that our governments have banned books in the past, burned copies of them, and even tried to prosecute their authors for indecency. This is more than an attack against our artwork or an attack against the artist: it is an attack against you, me, and everyone who would dare risk being who we are in a state bent on total, abject conformity.

It seems that sex is the hottest topic when it comes to literary censorship if only because the most famous banned books of the past century had some kinky parts to them. I personally find it hysterical that our government would ban any book that would have probably been celebrated in Ancient Rome, or would have been regarded as a national treasure had its author been born in another country; which has been the case in the past. I say this because all law and legality is relative, even within our own state. A misdemeanor in one country is a capital offense in some distant land. A sexual right in one state is outlawed in another. I see so many examples of artistic masterpieces, fantastic creations and achievements of the human body, unfairly labeled as pornography when some of the greatest artists in history would have found an amphitheater for them. I seriously wonder what the hell is wrong with us when we hold one book as one of the greatest in our national register while holding a pen to censor it.

The Muses do not discriminate based on social norms or language. They exist to inspire us in whatever form they see fit. They have gifted us with a fantastic power that can make us outlive our own lives: to become immortalized in the annals of history.

This is more than our right to express. This is our right to live. This is our right to leave a legacy for future generations, and every single one of our creations ripples through our society like pebbles in a pond. Our ripples are part of the great, complicated ocean of the human experience, yet the state is bent on fighting these natural currents with all their might if they so much as disagree with them.

They cannot destroy this current. As long as we, the living, live, we will continue to create. The state may continue to disagree with us, but they will remain on the losing side of history.

V

"One word: Crucifixion."
– Caiaphas

Censorship comes in many different forms. They have censored books due to subject matter and language, and statues due to their natural organs. They have censored public artwork due to their lack of paperwork, and have taxed, bullied, and even arrested street performers. However, very few subjects anger me more than the subject of music censorship. Music is the single highest form of human expression, and even if its songs do not speak for everyone, its collected work speaks for humanity.

Firstly, I find it difficult to take any nation seriously when it bears a list of "forbidden songs." Think about that for a minute. Picture it: a land where you are supposedly free to speak and write, but not to sing a certain tune. It doesn't make sense, does it? To make music is to be human! This is our speech! This is our story! This is our single, greatest voice! The entire world is in harmony on this one subject: we all love to sing!

To this day some of our politicians speak about music with disdain; how it leads to violence, murder, rape, insanity, stupidity, laziness, and possibly even the destruction of society. Dear reader, don't believe these lies. There has been no shortage of rape, war, and genocide at any time in our history, and I am pretty damn sure that music was not the cause of it. Was Abel inventing rap at the moment his brother killed him? Was Cleopatra a little bit too fond of pop? Was Attila too into punk? Were the Mongols just a rock concert? It is silly to entertain these notions, although

I will admit I am enjoying it.

Censoring music is a fool's attempt to make reason, to attempt at erasing a human vice as effortlessly as a word. I have stated this before: we are very cruel, dangerous creatures. We all have the ability in us to do great good and great injustice to our fellow man. I have no doubt that there are certain vices within us that require the strength of others to contain, but I do not believe that any of us posses the right or even the ability to destroy another part of each other.

Music is a part of us and perhaps the greatest part of us, and anyone who waxes about its evils might as well hold up a candle during a hurricane. Music is the single, universal language of this planet, and it does not need to be completely understood in order to be appreciated.

In fact, as a social experiment, I challenge every single nation on this planet to assemble their censored works and distribute them amongst themselves. Make it so that each nation possesses songs that cannot possibly be understood. Let the language of one song be completely foreign to the country that receives it. Let all the nations of the world listen to their most dangerous, forbidden work, and you will see that, for a moment, the world will be at peace...

At peace, listening to each other's forbidden music.

However, in a world such as ours, something tells me that just imagining this would be dangerous.

VI

"Video games are an even greater plight to our society than people who disagree with me."
— Sen. Joel Lüngermann

All right, let's settle this in one sentence: Video games are art, they should be regarded as such, and they must be protected as such.

End of story.

[Later]

All right, I admit that it is only fair for me to go into more detail about this.

Consider the collective talents that go into making a computer game: graphic art, concept art, storyboarding, scripting, voice acting, music, and direction. Every single one of these skills is an art in its own right, and they are all artists working on a collective project no differently than an actor sharing a stage or a musician in an orchestra. If anything, I see strength in their union, channeling their collective energies into a high art. I view video games as an art that encourages the audience to participate beyond their viewership or appreciation, but in their activity. This, my dear reader, is not simply a fine art or a high art: it is a great new kind of art. It is a fire that should be fanned instead of smothered, and I believe with all my heart that its creators' rights should be protected in full.

However, the state disagrees with me, and strongly so.

The state does not believe that video games are an art. If they did, there is no way they would have been able to get away with what they have.

The state believes that video games have become too mature and dangerous for our community. They have held committee hearings on them, debated them, and used all their powers to restrict their sales. They have attempted to link them to acts of violence just as hopelessly and desperately as the senator, congressman, or dictator who would dismiss art as degenerate.

They are fools. Lying, hypocritical fools.

Video games are an art, and they cannot be infringed upon. They are among our greatest artistic achievements and have ushered in a whole new form of entertainment, but they have not earned our respect. They have not earned support. Well, in my personal opinion, I don't think they need them. They don't need to be appreciated or legitimized any more in their community. Their status as works of art is self-evident, and nobody on this planet can take that away from them.

However, critics continue to take away their laurels and lawmakers continue to deny their right to exist. Such people should not be taken seriously. Instead, treat them like they don't exist and see how much they like it.

[Later]

Holy shit...[32]

---

32 http://arts.gov/grants/apply/AIM-presentation.html

VII

"I don't want my children seeing that, or anyone else's child."

– Fra Catalano

Vicious, cruel-hearted men have done everything within their power to scare society into submission by making our own artwork into an enemy. They have insulted us, cursed us, damned us to whatever hell they pleased, and twisted the truth like a dagger into the hearts of noble people. They have cast us off as crazies, predators, perverts, and inhumane. They have stripped us bare and flogged us in their arenas, destroyed our works in front of us, and done everything within their power to make us more like them.

They will not succeed.

The state will always fear artists, but we will never fear the state. No matter what they dismiss us as, we will always be in good company. No matter how much they censor, we will always have more to speak. No matter how much they destroy, we will always be able to create. The state fears us because they know that our work speaks to the public in ways they cannot duplicate. The artistic mind will always come out stronger when it has a greater cause to fight for than self-preservation. Artists speak to the masses as one of their own, not one of their inferiors. We are their vanguard, not their king. We work for them, not they for us. We are simply too unlike the state to ever conform to it, which is why they will always have to deal with us. No matter how the state chooses to subvert us, they will always be outmatched.

That is why so many dictators have always failed as artists.

Geometry

I

"Conquering the world... it never ends."
— Alexander

At long last, we come upon the end of our discussion. At long last, I can fall silent and allow myself to slip away...

But not yet.

There is one more mountain for me to climb in order to confront this government face-to-face, and that mountain is nothing short of the world that we all stand on. These are the stakes, my dear reader. This is how far the state has stretched its hands: around every corner of every continent in its insatiable lust for power.

Oh, how powerful the state has become in its false-flag attempt to make our own lives better. It has sent navies around the world, expanding its control like a Leviathan. It has outstretched its tentacles into foreign lands, killing friends and foes alike. It has slipped into the most secluded corners of this planet, orchestrating coup d'états, deposing leaders, and distributing arms to warring nations. It is everywhere and nowhere, ready to secretly strike at any enemy in the world...

Oh, but they did it all for us!

Our dear, sweet nanny knows that it was wrong to steal from neighbors just to feed us, to cheat children around the world just to clothe us and to murder millions around the world just to keep us safe. It knows that it did wrong, but the wrong was for a right! It did all this, for us, so that we could grow up in a better world.

This, my dear reader, is the lowest pit of the nanny state's treachery: the unspoken, endless war it has declared on the whole damn planet in our defense.

II

"We came, we killed, we colonized."
— John Smith Goodlove

Looking back, it is not all that difficult to see the origins of the nanny state even in the earliest pages in our history. After all, we have been so spoiled and swaddled and over-indulged our entire life that the only way we can live comfortably is at the expense of others.

Consider the conquest of our country: thievery, trickery, and murder. Our founders took more land than they ever could have needed, and possibly even more land than we need right now. They strong-armed us into wars so that we could accumulate more land, sent settlers to distant realms with the promise of free property, and ultimately turned ourselves into a continental power. We did not need to do this and it did not have to be our destiny, but our predecessors wanted it. They were determined to take as much as they possibly could in their mad grab for power.

Why did they do this? Why conquer all this land for us? Why turn us into an empire? What was their aim? What was their objective?

Why, obviously their own wealth.

The state did not give us welfare; they gave us bread and games. Those in power gave us pacifiers to shut us up while they carved an entire continent for themselves. They became some of the richest people to ever live, but it was all done at the expense of others. They created this country into a buffet and gave us just enough scraps to stave off starvation. However, we were truly the lucky ones, since it was everybody else who suffered. Our conquered subjects were dead and dying, and our purpose became imperial. We colonized the world, taking in much more than we ever needed to sustain ourselves. We did not ask for this or need this, but the state did it for us anyway. The state forced our soldiers into these wars, forced us into these distant lands, and ultimately forced us to live in a country that was built from the bottom-up on the suffering of others.

However, as I said, the state did all this for us! The state wanted us to live as well as we possibly could!

Well... not all of us. The state was slow to share this with everybody within our country, and ultimately was forced to make concessions based on race, sex, and creed. However, there is still one enormous factor that the state uses more than ever to seduce us into silence and compliance: the enormous wealth it brings us.

The wealthier you are in this land, the more the nanny loves you. She will give you just about anything you want and listen to your every wish. She will look the other way if you do wrong and promise not to ever, ever throw you in jail with all those bad people...

But like I said, she did this for us! She did this to show just how good life can be if we ever make it to the top! This was supposed to be our motivation; our urge to succeed. Just as our nation stepped on so many throats in order to stand as tall as it does, the nanny holds the most successful of us high in the air to spoils with endless gifts and attention.

This is our motivation. This is our spur.

In order to be one of our nanny's favorites--and yes, she does choose favorites--you have to be as merciless, cruel, and cold as she has always been.

III

"My laws are neither kind nor callous. My laws are justice as it is."

– Draco

Countries are inherently antagonistic creatures. As long as there are borders painted on this planet, I have no doubt that people will continue to fight over them. However, I think the invisible battlefield of the mind is where our planet is more vulnerable. After all, in the end aren't all wars fought simply because one party believes that the other party is wrong?

However, this chapter is not for discussing war or war fighting, but the danger posed by ideas, laws, doctrines, opinions made on the state level. It is virtually impossible for any nation, never mind any city, to put the full might of its people behind a single, unifying cause. Our nation, like so many nations, exercises the audacity to declare war, to authorize the use of sanctions, to try non-nationals in an international court. We even exercise the right to capture foreign fighters and torture them in our prisons; people who were not born here, don't belong here, and that our government has no purpose in its existence to stain our soil with the blood of. Our country exercises itself internationally, but it does not possess the right to. It almost drives me mad to picture our nation doing anything other than keeping itself to itself as much as possible.

I know that this sounds paranoid, but I am not talking about something as small as bumping your elbow into somebody. I am talking about ships sinking each other in disputed waters. I am talking about the implementation of something as impossible to define as international law. I am talking about something as oxymoronic as a just war.

Our nation has every right to be pissed off whenever people tell us what to do, so why are we allowed to play hall monitor? Why are we allowed to police the world? Why are we justified in dismissing civilian deaths as "collateral damage"? If somebody gets so much as a shin bruised due to our weapons, who are we to tell him that it's okay?

We are not. It is easy for out state to impose its political, legal, and military will on other countries because we enjoy the most powerful military alliances in the world. We are the ones who suffer least when we exercise the most force. We are the ones with every unfair advantage in the playbook. And, of course, when we win our battles, we are always the ones to call the terms. Unconditional surrender, total capitulation, military tribunals... how did this happen? How did we allow an invention as simple as the village turn into a new world order? Better us than them? Our might has made us so many enemies. Will they ever forgive us?

I don't know, but I know for sure that I will never forgive our state.

IV

"Only the strong shall inherit the Earth. The meek will inherit only enough to be buried in."
    – Sassol Mascheroni

We come to a subject that I had long wished to avoid if only because its maliciousness is so self-evident in just the mention of its name: genocide.

It is not easy to wipe an entire race of people off this planet. It requires time, energy, equipment, logistics, vehicles, weapons, and armies. It is not the kind of thing you do by accident, but a deliberate effort to change the world: an attempt to undo the miracle of humanity through the bluntest method possible--brute force. However, I hesitate to use those words because there seems to be nothing brute about it. After all, genocide requires a much more concerted effort than your typical brute has to offer. I attribute this partially to my earlier discussion about the hazardousness of a public school education. However, as cruel as brute force is, I view it as more of a small-scale threat to the human species. The larger, greater, and by far more destructive problem facing us is the intelligent force our nation--and, in truth, many nations--has used to deceive, displace, destroy, and ultimately depopulate a people. This, my dear reader, is the type of violence that should not be attributed to mere brutes. No. This is the type of annihilation that only a well-organized machine can set in motion. In this case, our own government.

There are few things that frighten me more than the human mind's potential for evil. While we may only have the will to make violence, it takes another, crueler person to calculate how best to use it. I am not speaking of war but of systematic, wholesale slaughter. I speak of the unpunished holocausts that have befallen too many people under our flag; I speak of the eradication of our native people; the enslavement of our brethren; the colonization of our neighbors; and the massacre of innocent men, women, and children half a world away. There are crimes against humanity on our conscience that we never could have performed had our state not forced us into the position where ordinary people are transformed into mass-murderers.

Ah, but I know what you are thinking: it was so long ago. Ask yourself, my dear reader: was it? Is a conquest or a massacre from two centuries past worth forgiving, forgetting, or even ignoring if there is not a single survivor alive? I find that a weak and pathetic excuse, and ultimately one rooted in one's own fear of reality. How would you feel if the holocausts and genocides from only 70 years ago were forgiven, forgotten, or even ignored in our lifetime? How about from 60 years ago? Or better yet, how about 38 years ago? You know, a wound from a long war so fresh that your parents could describe it in full detail... assuming they even remember the "incidents" of their lifetime. After all, it is easy to forgive an incident when it involves hundreds of federal units instead of soldiers, armored cars instead of horses, machine guns instead of rifles, grenade launchers instead of cannons,[33] and more than 130,000 rounds of ammunition.[34] It is easy to forget a conquest when our own government did the conquering. It is easy to ignore how one of the many tasks of this state is to maintain a martial law on its conquered subjects virtually indistinguishable

33 Howard Zinn, *A People's History of the United States* (New York: HarperCollins Publisher's Inc., 1999), 534.
34 Chrisopher J. Frey, "Native American Education," in *Encyclopedia of Educational Reform and Dissent, Volume II*, eds. James Carper, Thomas Hunt, Thomas Lasley, and C. Daniel Raisch, (Thousand Oaks: Sage Publications, 2010), 654.

from what it has in place for its citizens.

When I think about the difference just one life can make in this world, I have to pause and reflect upon how many times we screwed this planet over with our countless violent interventions. All our wealth and luxuries are nothing but a putrid pomp in comparison to the beauty I see in just one living person's eyes. I wish I could reach out and hold their hands, look deep into their souls, and witness for just one millisecond the millions of lights that so many cruel states have extinguished.

Instead, all I see is darkness. All around me. I look out and find the world a dimmer, quieter, lonelier place in their absence. I look to my left and right, but see nothing but empty space--which, sure enough, is just more nothing. I fold my arms, but still feel cold. I whisper, "Is anyone there?" only to be greeted by my own lonely echo.

This is the vast, empty country that our government helped create: a luxurious empire where the bourgeoisies can enjoy all the elbow room you could kill for. I think about this and become frightened about the trade our country made: an untold millions of human lives in exchange for loneliness.

Sure sounds to me like we got ripped off.

But I must hush now and continue to another subject before I lose myself in this cemetery.

V

"My one regret is that I probably won't live long enough
to witness the beauty of Armageddon."
                    – Bertran de Born

Nuclear war…

What is there to say about the subject that has not been
shared already? I know I am not the first person to write
about it, and I sure as hell won't be the last. Others have
taken much more intelligent, eloquent, and in some cases
hilarious approaches toward the subject, but I seem to have
a tough time talking about nuclear war without dying a
little on the inside.

I know that a lot of you are not very happy about the
thought of nuclear war. I also know that some of you can't
get enough of the subject if only because it is so difficult to
look away from it. I don't blame you for that. In fact, I would
say that is very human of you. Crazy shit like mushroom
clouds are sure to leave one hell of an impression on a
person, as would watching an entire flock of birds fry mid-
flight, a playground melt, or somebody getting turned into
a shadow.

That said, please accept the following information I was
able to gather on nuclear war:

Nuclear war sucks.

Fuck it.

Also, fuck everybody who made it possible.

…

There, I said it.

Also, I do feel a bit better right now.

Actually, on second thought, fuck it for all time because

I am still pretty pissed about all those missiles that the nanny maintains. You know, enough to usher in a second holocaust in the event of the slightest political, social, or even spiritual misunderstanding; enough to put the tens of millions of people located too closely to them in crosshairs for life; enough to threaten all plant and animal life on this planet; enough to make our government's efforts to curb nuclear research around the world all the more hypocritical; enough to make everybody on this world live in fear...

Just in case.

This was never your world to destroy, you damned nanny state. You are the harbinger of death to this planet. You are our living nightmare. You are what is wrong with humanity.

And all the worse, you are not even human.

VI

"Don't fuck with Earth."
– Giovanni Francesco di Bernardone

The nanny state is a blight upon these lands. It has outgrown its borders, spread like a cancer throughout the planet, and infected so many lives that even I am hard pressed to find the best course to confront it. However, there is one ally that we have working for us that I have no doubt will be able curb its power, destroy the state, and ultimately restore humanity to its pastoral roots. I speak, of course, of the planet Earth itself.

It is not much of a secret that just about every aspect of human achievement stands at the mercy of whatever natural calamity this planet chooses to unleash upon us. Pole shifts, tsunamis, and supervolcanoes and all natural occurrences of this planet, and the types of things that, in a strange, cruel way, sort of keeps the whole damn world we know in check. Life is all about interaction, and oh boy… have we been interacting with this planet. We have bulldozed its forests, polluted its oceans, stashed a bunch of radioactive material here or there, and shot such an untold amount of crap into the atmosphere that it seriously broke the sky. We have begun a mass extinction that we can proudly call our own, have shown no signs of stopping or slowing down, and have raised the oceans to the point that they are already starting to flood some of the most cherished cities on the planet. Still, the nanny state should not get blamed for this one. This was just humanity fucking up.

However, it would be nice if the nanny state had not

steered so close toward disaster in the first place. You know, such as by granting huge subsidies to oil companies so they could line our coast with bullshit oil rigs; looking the other way when businesses dumped chemicals into our water at fatal levels; and pretty much making it their job to keep the public from freaking out over real life shit like global warming. Personally, I don't give a damn about the oceans rising or hurricanes popping up where they shouldn't. The way I see it, this is nature's way of striking back at mankind with a one-two punch. However, I will object to some bullshit senator or congressman wasting our time and money by giving the scientific community the finger and telling the public this isn't happening. Yes, the evidence is all there. Yes, their findings seem real enough. And yes, you gotta be pretty stupid to disagree with it all.

Hey, Senator Old-White-Guy, you telling me that all this crazy shit isn't happening? You telling me this goddamn swarm of stink beetles was always in my house? You telling me that it isn't getting hotter every single damn year? You telling me that Mother Earth hasn't been acting a bit more pissy with us than usual these past few years? You tell me that every single nerd in the egghead business is wrong?

Please, give the Earth some credit. Of course global warming is real! Of course the planet's fucked! Yes, humanity took a stab at this planet and, well, we made some pretty big mistakes, but please don't insult our intelligence by suggesting that it doesn't exist! As if those last few "acts of God" were not enough of a wakeup call? Oh, I promise you, Mother Earth has shepherded this rock through a lot more serious shit than some old white guy from I-don't-give-a-fuck. I'm talking meteorites. Comets. Ice Ages. The kind of stuff that would do to civilization what Christianity did to Jesus: fucking destroy it. Oh yes, there is a very serious storm brewing, and I am willing to wager whatever you like that it will take down the nanny state with it. I don't know when it's going to come or what force of nature it takes the form of, but believe me when I say this: your days are numbered. Everything!

In all honesty, I'm somewhat in shock that you're still reading this. You and I have some serious work to do if we are to make it out of this fight alive, especially since the nanny state's solution to this mess is that we simply give it more power.

My dear reader, don't be played for a fool one second longer. Humanity needs you for something greater than your own death.

VII

"Death is life's dessert."
— Fra Alberigo

I have spoken to you as plainly and as truthfully as I can. I have shown you everything there is to know about our enemy so that you can emerge from this discussion more equipped to deal with it. I have given you everything I could have possibly asked for had I been in your position.

There is a storm coming, my friend, and I don't want it to end up being the end of life as we know it. You are not Noah or Jonah. No. You are someone much more important to this world: you are you. You are human. You are mortal. Just like everyone else, you too can drown in this storm. That is what we are up against in this struggle: humanity versus the nanny state. There can only be one survivor, and the winner inherits the world.

If the nanny state succeeds at its takeover, the world will end. Be it through conformity or war or aliens, the miracle of humanity will be over. The entire principle behind the nanny state is the surrender of some humanity for the sake of others. Dear reader, I have shown you the truth behind these lies and revealed how false this promise is. The nanny state is flawed and corrupt because that is how humans are. At the end, even our collective strengths were not enough to avoid building this mechanism in our own image. However, failure is the state's greatest weakness. It is the product of men. We, my dear reader, are the product of Earth.

We failed to improve upon ourselves, but I believe this is because we are such a miraculous creation to begin with.

We are the living and not the dead. We are humanity! Our mother was the single greatest engineer in the world, and we are her single greatest creation. We possess the power to do so much individually and as a whole that even at my weakest, darkest moments it is enough to give me hope. Never underestimate the power of human potential. We all share this world, and we all deserve the right to live in it as we see fit. I am so proud of this opportunity we have been in this life, and I will not let anything not born of its soil tell me what to do or how to live it. We are the natural! We are the born! The nanny state is the unnatural, the unborn, the inhuman. It is…

It is…

A non-entity.

My dear reader, my sweet friend, my equal, my brother… please, do not allow yourself to live in shackles for one minute more. The world needs more people like you, and so do I in the great fight to come. It will be long and hard, and I won't lie to you: this is a fight we could lose. However, risks can be useful if only because they make us assess our own value. You, my dear reader, are everything in the world to me, and all I ask is that you risk trusting me when I say this: Free yourself! Be yourself! Take back your freedom! I can only write about it: you alone can make it happen.

Reading this book, I will admit, was a pretty good start.

Thank you.

<u>17 Dante 17</u>